# GOOD WORDS ABOUT JESUS IN ALL FOUR SEASONS

Doc Hensley packs a punch but never preaches. An astounding amount of wisdom is found in these fast-paced chapters and scenes. It's entertainment with a purpose.

**Jon Gauger, interviewer, Moody Radio**

The only bad thing about *Jesus in All Four Seasons* is that it ends. Still, along the way it combines inspiration, hope, insight, passion, and motivation in pure Hensley fashion. He is a master writer, and this book is fresh, surprising, witty, and utterly entertaining.

**Bob Hostetler, author, *Falling in Love with God***

I don't hold a writers conference with asking Doc Hensley to speak. There is no one on the planet more powerful on the subject of communication than this man. I always tell listeners to fasten their seatbelts and be ready to take lots of notes. Well, with *Jesus in All Four Seasons*, Doc proves he knows whereof he speaks. Better tighten that seatbelt.

**Jerry B. Jenkins, author, *Left Behind***

*Jesus in All Four Seasons* is a GPS for life, capable of navigating anyone from desperation to destination. By revealing real-life lessons and interlacing them with energetic and introspective contemporary applications drawn from the teachings of Christ, Doc Hensley is nothing short of brilliant. The book is a must-read road map to successful living: it's educating, encouraging, and empowering!

**Joyce Oglesby, national talk show host, "Just Ask Joyce,"**
**WFIC radio, Louisville**

At the end of this phenomenal book, Dennis E. Hensley writes a scene so passionate, it brought me to tears. When Christ's earthly father Joseph, on his death bed, instructs his son about how to face death with dignity, purpose, and bravery, the tenderness of the father-son relationship is magnificent. This is storytelling with impact.

**Elizabeth Nulf MacDonald, TV talk show host,**
**"The Verbal Edge"**

# Jesus

## in All

## Four

## Seasons

# JESUS

## in All

# FOUR

## SEASONS

### HAVING CHRIST AS
### YOUR LIFE COACH

The Sequel to *Jesus in the 9 to 5*

Dennis E. Hensley, PhD

Bold Vision Books
PO Box 2011
Friendswood, Texas 77549

Published in association with MacGregor Literary Agency,
PO Box 1316, Manzanita, OR 97130

Cover photo by @nikolai Sorokin Four Seasons
Cover designed by *k*ae Creative Solutions
Interior designed by *k*ae Creative Solutions

Bold Vision Books
PO Box 2011
Friendswood, Texas 77549

Printed in the United States of America

# DEDICATION

This book is fondly dedicated to Larry and Janice Wehner, who have given us decades of love, laughs, and travel adventures. What a blessing you've been to us, friends!

To Joe Duncan,

I will always remember the energy you put into your presentation for senior capstone. You were funny, insightful and motivating. It has been a real joy to have you as my student.

Doc Hensley

# CONTENTS

## SECTION *1*

# NO EXCUSE FOR A LACK OF PROGRESS

I arrived in Vietnam on January 2, 1971. It took me just one week to figure out that only two kinds of soldiers were serving over there: those marking time, and those maximizing time. I was determined to be in the latter category.

Sixty men were in my "hootch," and we were not unlike the sixty guys in the hootch next to ours and the one next to it, *ad infinitum*. Walking through the rows of bunks and lockers, it became immediately evident to me that most of the men considered themselves to be in a state of personal limbo, marking off calendar days and going through the motions of daily existence until they could return to "the world" and get their lives back.

"You'll hate it here," my bunkmate, a corporal named Becker, told me as I began to transfer things from my duffle bag to my locker.

"Really?" I said. "How so?"

He stared at me as if I'd grown a third eye. "You're kidding, right?" he asked flatly. "Look around, man. We're fifteen thousand miles away from America, living in a snake and mosquito infested jungle, where the temperatures climb above a hundred every day during dry season or it rains sixteen hours a day in rainy season. Oh, yeah... and then there's that other little matter about there being forty thousand guys out there who want to kill us. This ain't Disneyland, pal."

"Ever read Milton?" I asked, turning to make up my bunk.

"Berle?"

"No," I said. "John Milton. The poet. He wrote *Paradise Lost*. He said that the mind is its own territory. Milton believed you could make a heaven of hell or a hell of heaven. It all depended on your frame of reference."

Cpl. Becker shook his head, dropped onto the lower bunk, and lit a cigarette. "Good luck on that one," he said with a wry grin. "At least you got the hell part right."

**Personal Accountability**

Later that night, as I lay in my bunk, I thought back to a week earlier when my family had driven me to Detroit to catch a flight to California, and thence to 'Nam. My father, a decorated naval veteran of World War II, had pulled me aside. "You remember everything we talked about while you were home on leave?"

"I do," I assured him. "I should use every opportunity to make this year away from the States a growing experience. No wasted time. Read, travel, use time wisely."

He nodded and smiled approvingly. "Good man. Keep a daily journal of your activities. Use it as a kind of scorecard to mark your progress. And send me letters, filling me in on everything you're involved in. I'll write to you every day, even if it's just to send you clippings from the hometown newspaper or a church bulletin. I remember what it felt like to go to mail call and have nothing. That won't be you. Trust me."

"I do trust you," I said.

He hugged me vigorously for a long time, then released me. The last thing he said was, "There is no excuse for a lack of progress, under any circumstances. I know you'll do well at whatever you set your mind on. This can be a great year for you."

I'll admit that being levied to serve a year in Vietnam at age twenty-two had not been the Christmas present I had been hoping for in 1970. I had graduated from college in December 1969, worked for six months in my hometown of Bay City, Michigan, and then enlisted in the Army in June. I'd spent the previous seven months stateside with the armor corps at Fort Knox, Kentucky.

I was made a chaplain's assistant, and at Fort Knox it was a rather plum job. I would type correspondence, answer the phone, drive the chaplain to his rounds at the hospital, set up counseling appointments, and clean the chapel. Sure, I had to do combat training with tanks one day per week, but that wasn't so bad. However, in Vietnam it was a different story. Chaplains don't bear arms, even in a combat zone, so the chaplain's assistant must serve as a bodyguard. Thus, I was assigned to the 284th Military Police Company and, worse yet, was attached to a chaplain who worked twelve hours per day inside of a military prison. Yeah…as if being in a war zone wasn't bad enough.

They had given me a ten-day leave to go home before being sent to 'Nam. My mother had been terrified about me going to a war zone for twelve months. The whole time I was home, she couldn't sleep at nights, always pacing and wringing her hands and crying. My dad, however, had a completely different take on the situation. To him, life itself was a bit of a war, and if you knew more than your enemy, you'd come out the victor. For a fact, a *real* war provided opportunities for greater focus and concentration on personal advancement.

"This prison assignment is going to be a blessing," my father said to me one day while I was still in Michigan. "John Bunyan, Ghandi, Martin Luther, even Martin Luther King, Jr. all did their best writing while in prison.

The Bible is filled with prison champions—Joseph, Daniel, Paul, Peter. Yep, this assignment to do duty in a prison can really work in your favor."

I'll admit, I was hard-pressed to be as optimistic about what lay ahead of me, but my father was adamant about it being a time of golden opportunities.

## A Heaven of Hell

To save time, let me cut to the summary. By taking military correspondence school courses, I was promoted twice while in Vietnam, ending my twelve-month tour as a Specialist Fifth Class (noncommissioned officer, E-5). I took evening classes in tae kwon do from our Korean allies and earned a brown belt after ten months. I met each afternoon with a Vietnamese officer; he taught me Vietnamese, and I taught him English. We had a base library, so I was able to read an average of three books per week the whole year I was overseas. I spent time at the arms range and qualified on the grenade launcher, .45 automatic pistol, and 60mm machine gun. I watched fifty-four movies that year (albeit that the screen was a bed sheet and the reels had to be changed at intervals because we had only one projector.) And, I did my regular work so conscientiously, I was awarded five Letters of Commendation, six medals, and two unit citations. I used my one week of R & R and one week of leave to travel to Thailand and then to Taiwan.

My father was ecstatic about my letters home. He would write back or send me a cassette tape and say, "Excellent! Excellent! Not a week goes by that you're not learning something new or advancing yourself in some way. Opportunities for advancement are always available, under any circumstances. Keep up the good work."

Regrettably, Cpl. Becker and others of his ilk squandered their time in Vietnam. They arrived with an attitude of defeat, saw nothing positive about the situation, and left a year later eager to resume watching TV, eating junk food, and hanging out with friends.

Many years later I occasionally would cross paths with some of the guys I'd served with. It was interesting to see the results of an early pattern set in life. Those, like me, who had been opportunists in Vietnam had also become opportunists back in America, and they had risen to high ranks in business, academia, or in a professional calling. However, those who had marked time in 'Nam hadn't fared all that well stateside either. They had remained blind to openings, options, and chances for advancement, even though such opportunities had been bountiful.

**Regaining Paradise**

These days, as I reread the daily journal I kept while in Vietnam, I'm not really surprised to discover that the lessons written there, given to me by my dad, have withstood the test of time. Let me share a few with you:

**Find mentors.** Whether you're the new guy at the factory, the new gal at the daycare center, or the intern at the corporate office, you can learn something from anyone who has been at the job longer than you have.

Ask questions. Listen carefully. Take notes. Seek advice. Most senior employees are willing to share their experience and guidance with someone who is sincerely inquisitive and respectfully grateful for help. Latch onto these folks and draw tips and direction from them.

**Read voraciously.** Printed books, recorded books, and screen-displayed books provide a wide range of learning experiences. Make use of your area school libraries and public libraries. One college student had the boring job of working at a payment booth at a city parking lot for the summer. Customers often left their cars all day, so the young man used the uninterrupted time to read self-help books and classic novels. Night watchmen, people making transcontinental flights, folks traveling cross-country by train, evening babysitters, and Maytag® repairmen use time on their hands to advance themselves by reading.

**Barter services and skills.** Two firefighters, one in his late forties and the other in his early twenties, often went for days just sitting at the firehouse when there were no fires or accidents to attend to. To make better use of their time, the younger man brought in a laptop and helped the older man increase his computer skills. The older man brought in an easel and paints and taught the younger man how to create watercolor landscapes.

***Take on additional assignments.*** A warehouse worker often found himself with three or four hours of "wait time" until new trucks would arrive that needed to be unloaded. He asked his supervisor how he could make himself more useful to the company. Soon, the man was being taught bookkeeping skills, how to gauge inventory, and how to file insurance claims for broken or missing shipments. His strong work ethic, combined with his range of new skills, made him first in line when an extra warehouse manager needed to be hired.

***Start an exercise regimen.*** Invigorating the body not only tones muscles, but it also sends more oxygen to the brain, thus stimulating creative thinking. A woman worked one summer on a cruise ship. Each morning she would call out bingo numbers for three hours. After lunch she would sit for four hours as the ship's librarian. The work was so sedentary it would have driven the woman crazy, except that she started to get up very early each morning and attend a fitness class offered by the ship's recreational director. At nights she would also take two laps around the ship after dinner. She found that walking not only helped her lose weight and improve her heart rate, but it also gave her time to plan and think insightfully about her future.

***Expand your cultural experiences.*** A concert violinist at a social event was once absolutely astounded when he met a farmer who could talk at great length about classical music. The farmer explained to the musician that he was required to spend endless hours in the cab of his tractors and combines in order to plant and harvest his crops. He used the time to listen to symphonic orchestras. One season he did baroque music, another time chamber music, and military marches the next.

## Learning Opportunities Abound

In Daniel Defoe's 1719 novel, *Robinson Crusoe*, the title character was isolated for more than twenty years on a deserted island. He created a calendar, developed a garden, hued out a gondola, learned to weave baskets and hats and mats from local vegetation, captured animals, and designed and built a home. No matter what circumstances a person finds himself or herself in, there are always opportunities to learn new skills and make progress in life. Look for those opportunities. If they aren't immediately evident, then use the tactics found in this section to *create* opportunities. Remember that the mind is its own territory. Make yours a heavenly place to be.

# Key Points Found in Section *1*

1. There is no excuse for a lack of progress, under any circumstances.

2. The mind is its own territory. You can make a hell of heaven or a heaven of hell, depending on your outlook and attitude.

3. People who are opportunists under the worst circumstances will certainly be opportunists under the best of circumstances.

4. Find mentors, ask questions, listen carefully, and take notes.

5. Read voraciously. A school or public library contains a wealth of information.

6. Barter services and skills. Learn something by offering to teach something.

7. Take on additional assignments. Master new skills and move up the ladder.

8. Start an exercise regimen. Exercise can be done anywhere, and it has both physical and mental benefits.

9.  Expand your cultural experiences. Art, music, languages, crafts, travel, and dance can be studied, learned, and experienced via books, recordings, DVDs, or lessons.

*Stepping out of the glare of the TV talk show spotlights, the assistant director asked, "Is our second guest out of make-up yet?"*

*"He didn't want to be touched," answered Liz, the staff cosmetologist. "His name's Johnny Wildman, and he looks the part. Wait till you see him—scruffy beard, desperately in need of a haircut, camel-hair sport coat but no tie, blue jeans, and sandals. They say he's a college professor, but you could've fooled me."*

*"He's a maverick, all right. Teaches economics at some West Coast school. He wrote this book five years ago."* *She held up a hardbound text with the title* <u>The Profitless Corporation vs. the Prophetless Corporation</u>. *"He predicted someone would come along and create a business model where the focus of making a profit would be to provide beneficial services to society. Critics labeled him a nutcase, except now, some guy's started a furniture company, and he's actually managing the place using those very principles. Successfully, too. Ergo, Professor Wildman is now being called, by some, a visionary, and everyone wants him on the talk show circuit."*

*"How'd we get him?"*

*"Turns out, Mildred was a former student of his before*

*he got the boot from some Ivy League university. She called him, and he agreed to be on the show." The AD glanced at her clipboard of to-do items. "Oh, did you offer him a bottle of water or some throat lozenges before going on?"*

*"He passed. Said he had some packets of honey he preferred."*

*"Hmmm. Well, whatever works. Okay, bring him out. Have one of the tech boys get him seated and miked. We start taping the second half of the show in five minutes. Let's hope this section is livelier than what we just taped. Did you see them? Couple of real estate speculators. Husband and wife. Ananias and Sapphira. Sounds like a vaudeville act. Where do we dig up these people?"*

*In short order, Johnny Wildman was brought onto the set and seated before a trio of cameras. The staged setting featured a couple of potted plastic trees, a painted ocean backdrop, and a colorful banner emblazoned with* **MONEY WISE.** *Seated opposite him was a smartly dressed woman of about thirty.*

*"Comfy?" she asked.*

*"Actually, I'm more of a desert person," said Wildman, waving at the backdrop, "but at least these lights are giving us the heat effect."*

*The host now looked directly into the center camera as her peripheral vision watched her show's director do a raised finger countdown from five to zero.*

23

*"Good day, everyone, and welcome back to the second half of this edition of 'Money Wise.' I'm your host, Mildred Franklin. Joining me is Dr. Johnny Wildman, professor of business and economics at Clara Barton Community College in Desert Vista, California. Dr. Wildman was a guest on this program five years ago, just after the release of his highly controversial book. He predicted the rise of companies that would exist solely for the benefit of society. At that time, Dr. Wildman was the chair of the economics department at a major East Coast university. However, after his book riled many of the profit-based corporate donors who supported that university, Dr. Wildman's contract was not renewed... something I recall making a prediction about back then."*

*Johnny Wildman leaned forward, nodded amiably, and interjected, "I believe your exact words, Milly, were something to the effect of, 'If you continue to espouse the birth and expansion of profitless corporations, they'll have your head on a platter, Johnny.'"*

*Turning slightly, Mildred Franklin jumped right to the crux of the interview. "Everyone on Wall Street—and Main Street, for that matter—is talking about the success of Tree of Life Furnishings. The products are innovative, well-built, reasonably priced, and very functional. But the CEO says he has no plans to take the company public. For a fact, whatever profits the company makes wind up being donated to orphanages, soup kitchens, and free medical and dental clinics.*

*So, tell me, this CEO, who goes by just one name, Jesus, is he
the one you predicted in your book would come along and
change the face of modern capitalism?"*

*"He's a piece of work, isn't he?"*

*Mildred paused, then said, "You seem entertained by
this. However, I'm wondering why you aren't outraged. I reread
your book this past week, and this Jesus seems to have read it,
too. He's instituted your systems, your management goals, even
your concept of giving away all earnings."*

*Johnny Wildman shook his head. "No...no, not at all.
My book is a collection of concepts, thoughts, and theories. I
put forth a new business model for organizations that would
exist only to deploy their excess cash flow to 'the least among
us.' I summarized the collective ways folks banded together to
survive during the Great Depression. I presented documentation
supporting the idea that companies that earmark portions of
their earnings to be given to charitable organizations usually
benefit greatly from the positive public relations this generates
for the company's image and reputation." He raised a hand.
"But don't confuse an economics professor like me with a hands-
on leader like Jesus. He has truly given form and substance to
my abstract thoughts and concepts. When he walked into my
office, I wanted to get down and spit-shine his shoes."*

*Mildred's eyebrows rose. "He came to see you? He
actually came to your office?"*

*"Yeah, I know what you're thinking. Surprised the
heck out of me, too, but there he was. He told me I had paved*

*the way for him, and he thanked me. I laid out my situation before him, told him the truth, that I'd been banished to the wilderness after I'd published my book, and even though I'd continued to spout the same rhetoric, very few people were really listening to me, much less taking me seriously as an economic theorist. He actually chuckled at that and said something about prophets not being appreciated in their own hometowns."*

*"But what was his purpose in coming to see you? Did he have some kind of agenda?"*

*"Nope. In fact, from my perspective, it was a waste of his time."*

*"How so?"*

*Wildman shrugged and looked self-consciously at the floor. "I know this is going to sound crazy, but he said he came to see me so he could attend one of my classes…so he could become 'immersed' in what I was offering to everyone else."*

*"Was he serious or mocking you?"*

*"He doesn't do anything unkind," Wildman responded, almost defensively. "Trust me, he was serious all right. But, naturally, I felt inferior to him. I mean, sure, I'd written a book about profitless corporations, but he'd actually put such a corporation together. I told him that he ought to be the guest speaker that day and that I should have a seat and let him teach me."*

*A side camera positioned itself to get a close-up of both the host and the interviewee.*

*"Did Jesus accept your offer?"*

*"He did not. Instead, he walked down the hall, entered the classroom, sat in the front row, and paid close attention to everything I taught that hour. The other students kept looking over at him, wondering why a guy like that would be coming to me for lessons in something he was already the master of. But, parenthetically, I've got to tell you that since that day, I've gotten more respect and more attention from my students than ever before. I mean, when this guy endorses you, it changes your life."*

*"So, are you thinking he is the living, breathing, in-the-flesh CEO you predicted would one day come forth to change the way we think about business?"*

*Johnny Wildman considered that a moment, and Mildred gave him time to prepare his thoughts. Her producer was mouthing the words "dead air," but she ignored him. She knew that whatever Dr. Wildman said next would be the high point of this interview, and she was hoping to get a response that might wind up as sound bites on dozens of news broadcasts worldwide. This had the potential of being a career-making moment for her.*

*"Okay, let me try to explain my take on this," Wildman began at last. "That day when Jesus was leaving our campus, he went outside. A weird thing happened. Our school mascot is the turtledove, and we keep a dove outside on display. We call her Lovey-Dovey. Corny, I know, but my point is, somehow*

*Lovey's cage had gotten knocked over that morning, and she had flown away. It was some kind of an accident by one of the maintenance workers. Everyone was sad about this because Lovey had some special markings on her wings that made her <u>our</u> school bird. It set her apart, and now we'd lost her. But as Jesus walked outside, that bird appeared out of nowhere and came floating down onto his shoulder. He reached over, moved it to his hand, carried it back over to the cage, stroked its head, and then put it back inside. I can't tell you why, but all of us who witnessed that scene had a feeling that this guy was…well, was like in tune with nature…in tune with everything. It was like he had the whole world in his hands. And I suddenly had this revelation that what he was doing at that furniture company was only a small part of what this guy was all about."*

*"You're saying he wasn't 'business as usual' in more than one sense," suggested Mildred.*

*"Actually, I just didn't know what to make of it," admitted Wildman. "I spent the next week reading all I could find about him, stuff that had been printed in newspapers and magazines and on blogs. None of it got to the core of what I was trying to figure out. So, I took a more direct step"*

*"Which would be…?"*

*"I called the HR director of Tree of Life Furnishings. I asked if it would be possible for me to send four of my graduate students, all business majors, to spend a week working at the*

*plant and at their offices, just trying to get a feel for how things operated. I wanted them to get a chance to tweak the CEO's brains, too. The HR director said okay, and she even found places for these students to stay. I briefed the students before they left."*

Mildred leaned slightly closer. "What did you say to them?"

"Well, naturally, I told them to take good notes, make photos, meet a lot of people. But my paramount instruction was for them to ask Jesus point blank, 'Are you the incarnate CEO whom Johnny wrote about?' I wanted to know, once and for all, if my business philosophies and theories were actually functional, actually doable. I'd convinced myself that if anyone could fill those shoes—shoes I wasn't even worthy of tying, I might add—it was this man. But I needed to know if he believed he was that man."

"And what happened?"

Johnny smiled. "It turned out, the students didn't even get to see him until the last day they were there. They were kept busy prior to that. They were in the warehouses, in the accounting offices, at the shipping and receiving docks, at the assembly lines, even in the lunchrooms. They taped hours of interviews, shot hundreds of photos."

"Yes, yes," said Mildred, "but did they get a chance to ask the big question?"

"Yes…and no," replied Johnny. "On Friday afternoon before wrapping up their week, they were brought to the CEO's *office. Jesus asked them how they had enjoyed their week. The students—two guys and two gals—showed him all their research data and talked about their experiences. And then, before they could pose my question, Jesus said, 'So, let me ask you, do you think what we are doing here is a working model of what your professor wrote about in his book five years ago?' And this caught the students flat-footed, because he'd turned the tables on them."*

*"I understand from what I've read about him that he's known for that kind of thing."*

*"True, true. But reading about it being done to someone else and having it done to you, personally, is something very different. The students had to take a few minutes to formulate their answers."*

*"And what did they say?"*

*"Ultimately, they said they were going to go back and tell me all that they had observed. And not just about ergonomics and budgets and shipping manifests. They were going to tell me stories. Stories about the people whose lives have been changed by being around this man."*

*"Such as...?"*

*"Such as a guy named Pete Fishers who told them he was a drunk without a dime to his name until Jesus pulled him out of a bar, gave him a job with serious responsibility, and radically altered his life. And a story about a guy named Matt Feingold, who had been an IRS agent, closing down people's businesses because they couldn't pay their taxes, until Jesus*

*called him away from that and put him into an environment where he could use his skills to make jobs for people. About a woman named Juanita, whose marriage was saved and whose friendships were restored...about a young salesman named Jonathan Markelson who was given a life-changing second chance to get back on the right track...and about a guy named Paul Stoner, who...."*

*"Whoa! Whoa!" interrupted Mildred. "This is only a fifteen-minute segment, Dr. Wildman." She laughed good naturedly, but deftly redirected the conversation to the issue at hand. "So, you're saying that this iconoclastic CEO is as much a social worker as he is a business magnate?"*

*"What I'm saying is, from this point on, people should throw my book away and, instead, focus on this man. I'm not important anymore. I need to fade from the spotlight, and he needs to be given center stage. Now that he's here, establishing a cultural arena where people can put others first, we need to learn all we can from this man. Yeah, he's part social worker, part businessman, but he's a whole lot more. Hard to find the words for it."*

*Mildred allowed a beat for dramatic flair, but then gave a subtle nod to a side cameraman, who instantly recognized the cue and moved his lens for a full-face close-up of Mildred Franklin.*

*"Well, viewers, you've heard it straight from the source—Dr. Johnny Wildman, himself. He claims that altruistic capitalism can work and, for a fact, is working at Tree of*

*Life Furnishings. But, alas, once again, as I did five years ago, I feel compelled to raise a voice of concern…indeed, a voice of dire warning."*

*Again, she allowed a beat of time for dramatic effect. "I've spent my entire professional life interviewing corporate tycoons, profiling billionaire entrepreneurs, and entering into dialogues with stock traders. Regretfully, but realistically, I must say I've seen precious little emphasis on building companies and corporations for the benefit of giving away all the earnings. In fact, and I say this with a heavy heart, for Dr. Wildman was actually one of my own professors some ten years ago and has been a role model for me ever since, I predict that both Johnny Wildman and Jesus are doomed to a bad end because of good intentions. I hope I'm wrong, but I live in the real world, where it pays to be money wise. So long for today, friends."*

*Theme music rose and credits rolled on screen. After thirty seconds the director could be heard yelling, "We're clear. Much better second half, everyone. Let's break the set."*

*Johnny Wildman fiddled with removing his lapel mic. "Well, you were the voice of optimism, weren't you?" he said.*

*Mildred Franklin didn't rise to the sarcasm. "You didn't listen to me five years ago, Dr. Wildman, and I'm sure you aren't going to listen to me today. But we both know that if you keep promoting these ideals about profitless businesses, there are bad people out there who are going to bury you. And your pal Jesus."*

*Johnny stood and dropped the mic on his seat. "You may be right, but I've never felt more sure about anything in my whole life. And if it spells my doom, then so be it. But I've got to tell you something." He smiled with genuine kindness for her concern. "If the bad guys, as you predict, really do bury Jesus, I have a feeling he will find a way to rise above it. Just a hunch, mind you, but I really think he will."*

*He reached into his sport coat pocket, extracted a small packet of honey, tore it open, and squeezed the contents into his mouth. He waved as he moved off set and disappeared from the spotlights.*

## SECTION 2

## EAT LESS AND MOVE MORE

I saw a cartoon once of a guy sitting in a chair reading a book called *The Eat All You Want Diet.* The guy was turned toward his wife and saying, "I knew there had to be a catch. You have to walk 150 miles every day."

Yep, you've got that right. Exercise programs and fad diets come and go continually. I have heard about jazzercising, jogging, running, rolling on a large ball, skipping rope, bouncing on miniature trampolines, following weight-lifting regimens, using a variety of health club machines, trying karate kicks to disco music, and experimenting with isometrics. The diets have included counting calories, measuring grams of fat, ingesting brown rice, drinking eight glasses of water a day, swallowing vitamin and mineral supplements, fasting, eating seven small meals instead of three large meals, chewing each bite of food forty times, and stocking up on carbohydrates while ignoring fat and protein.

I'll confess that at various times of my life, I've experimented with a few of these diets, and, in most instances, had temporary success with them. What I discovered was not very profound. Every diet works. One is not really better than another. Likewise, every exercise program works. They are all designed to increase muscle tone and improve cardiovascular endurance. Big surprise, eh? It turns out that the key to success at losing weight and getting into condition is discipline.

I know this latter statement to be true, because I once had it forced upon me. While in college as an English major, I sat around a lot reading books. I drove places in my used Mustang. I wasn't part of any college sports team. I lived by the simple motto of, "No pain...no pain." And then I enlisted in the United States Army.

I never liked mornings, but my drill sergeant felt that 5:00 a.m. was a great time to rise, even if I wasn't shining. We trainees had breakfast, if anyone was in the mood, and then it was off for an invigorating five-mile run, following by calisthenics, and then classroom sessions, followed by lunch, followed by a long hike, followed by hand-to-hand combat training, followed by dinner, followed by three hours of cleaning weapons, shining boots, fixing footlockers, cleaning the barracks, hitting the showers, and then studying the basic training manual. After three months of this regimen, I had lost twenty-four pounds and was leaner and in better shape than at any time in my life.

This is not to say I didn't hate every minute of it. However, it is to say that people are out of shape because they *don't* exercise and they *do* eat too much. True, there are exceptions in any situation, and I'm sure there are people with certain disorders that make them more apt to become obese, but, for most of us, blubber is self-generated.

## So, What Are My Options?

When I moved to the town of North Manchester, Indiana, in 1978, my wife and I went in to register for a new family doctor. The nurse said, "Did you have any one of our staff doctors in mind?"

I said, "Who is the fattest one?"

The nurse blinked and asked me to repeat my question, which I gladly did. She stammered a bit and finally said the name of a certain young doctor who was "slightly rotund." Turned out, when I met him, he was at least fifty pounds overweight for his height. I knew right away this guy and I would get along.

And for two years we did. He never bugged me about annual physicals or losing weight or exercising. If I had a cold, I would go in, he'd look down my throat, write me a prescription, and I'd be gone. But then the doc's insurance carrier started jacking up rates on its high-risk clients, which included physicians. Unless the doc got in shape, he was going to be paying rates on a par with his malpractice insurance. He didn't want that, so he joined "The Tub Club." He started a walking ritual each evening, cut back on starches and fats, and soon was starting to drop pounds. And guess what that did for our relationship? Yeah, exactly. Next thing I know, he's giving me lectures about heart disease and telling me to start working out.

I explained that when I came home from the war in Vietnam, I had sworn off hikes and other outdoor activities. If I never had to negotiate another jungle, swamp, mountain, river, or gorge the rest of my life, I would be okay with that. He smiled and said, "Then play."

"Say again?" I asked.

"Play," he repeated. "Take up a sport or an outdoor game or some kind of mildly stimulating activity, have some fun at it, and don't call it exercise. Just be consistent at it. As long as you get your heart pumping and you burn some calories, that's all that counts."

So, my wife and I joined a church indoor volleyball group. It was just a bunch of middle-agers like ourselves who played scratch games with whomever showed up a couple of times a week, but it was fun and cheap, and at the end of four games, we had broken into a pretty good sweat. And, coincidentally, I started dropping a few pounds. (I think after playing each night, I was too tired to lift the potato chips to my mouth.)

**Recognizing the Bad Habits**

The next time I saw my family physician, he and I both had lost some weight. I told him about the volleyball, and he was pleased. Then he shared another easy tip.

"Pay attention to the bad habits," he advised me. "If you've had a full dinner, do you really need a bowl of pretzels when watching TV? Probably not. But if you cannot stop cold turkey, to use an appropriate metaphor, and you need to wean yourself from the munching habit, swap out the pretzels for some crunchy raw cauliflower or celery sticks. In time, TV and eating won't be simultaneous actions in your mind."

I also would catch myself doing a lot of "bonus" eating when making long trips in the car…working at the computer…sitting and reading a book. I worked at breaking those eating habits, too. To no surprise, I was able to drop even more pounds.

The big discovery for me was that my doctor had not suggested I use the Atkins Diet or the Scarsdale Diet or the South Beach Diet, good though each one of these plans might be in its own way. What he had said was to "play" (move more) and eliminate the bad eating habits (eat less). It was, actually, that simple. And, it still is.

# Key Points Found in Section *2*

1. Most people are overweight because of poor eating habits and a lack of exercise.

2. Changing the term "exercise" to "play" can be motivating in trying to do more physical activity during the week.

3. Having a spouse or friend join with you in your workout enhances the enjoyment.

4. Even just changing a few habits, such as eating better snacks, can make a major improvement in your health.

5. Any good diet will work, but each one ultimately will come down to eating less and moving more.

*Jesus closed the folder in front of him. "I think that does it, unless you three have something else to cover." He pushed his chair back slightly from his desk.*

*Martha, Pete, and Matt shook their heads and began to gather up their electronic tablets and other paraphernalia.*

*"Good. Then I'm heading down to our break room to see if I can have lunch with Danielle," said Jesus.*

*"What? That skinny little internship girl?" said Pete. "Ugh! I can't stand that kid."*

*"What's your beef against her?" asked Matt.*

*"That girl's weird, with a capital W," insisted Pete. "I've kept my distance from her ever since last summer's company picnic. What a killjoy."*

*Martha wrinkled her brow and set her tablet back on the desk. "I think she's a bit reclusive, but she's remarkably intelligent. I don't know why you wouldn't like her. Of the four recent high school graduates in our three-year work-study program, Danni is our top student. She takes classes at the community college and puts in twenty hours a week for us. She's as sharp as they come."*

*"I want nothing to do with her," Pete said. "Last summer for some children's entertainment at the company*

*picnic, I hired a juggler, a clown, and a magician. Each time the magician did a trick, this Danielle turns to the kids and says, 'There is no such thing as magic. He moved one hand to make you look away, and then he used the other hand to slide the ball off the table. So, there is no ball under any of the three cups now. It's not magic. It's just a trick. There are no magic people or astrologers or anybody who can do anything except trick you. Don't fall for it.'" Pete shook his head. "I mean, one trick right after another, she's figuring out how the guy is doing it, and she's explaining it to the kids. The guy doing the tricks wasn't any too happy, either."*

*Matt chuckled. "Hilarious! I missed that."*

*"Not funny," insisted Pete. "I went over and nudged little Danni-girl by the elbow and directed her away from the magician, and I said I'd go get her a hotdog. But she tells me that she can't eat no hotdog because she's a fan of* <u>Star Trek</u>.*"*

*"That's* <u>not</u> *what she said," Martha cut in. "I was there. What she said was, she couldn't eat a hotdog because she was a vegan."*

*Pete shrugged. "Vegan…Vulcan…whatever. I still say anyone who swears off hotdogs is a weirdo."*

*"I'm not sure I know who she is," said Matt.*

*"Not surprised," said Pete. "She's always either hiding behind a computer screen or buried in some book. She's short, wears her hair in kind of an old-fashioned bob, doesn't weigh more than eighty-five pounds soaking wet, and wears eyeglasses*

*that look like magnifiers. Sweet little Danielle Beltzer. To use a baseball metaphor, that is one kid who's out in left field."*

*"Metaphor?" echoed Martha. "Since when do you know the meaning of the word* <u>metaphor</u>*?"*

*"Since when do you know the meaning of* <u>left field</u>*?" countered Pete.*

*Jesus pointed a pencil toward Matt. "Ah! See? I said that spending more time with you would be beneficial to him."*

*Pete faced the group. "I still say, someone needs to point that Danielle in a new direction."*

*Jesus gave a wink to Matt and Martha. "Someone will." He left the office.*

*"Is it interesting?"*

*Danielle, sitting at a lunchroom table, looked up from her book to see Jesus standing opposite her. He eased onto the bench, opened a sack, and withdrew an orange.*

*"The book? Yes, sir...some of it, anyway." She allowed Jesus to reach across and take the book from her hand.*

*He examined the spine, nodded, and gave it back to her. "Freud's writings on dream interpretation. Is that an area of interest of yours?" He began peeling his orange.*

*"It's for a class I'm taking in psychology," said Danielle, "but I've always been fascinated by dreams, figuring out what*

*they mean. I have to say I don't always agree with Freud's explanation of dreams. Well, except for one part. I think he was right when he said sometimes, even in a dream, a cigar is nothing more than a cigar."*

*"I like that, too," said Jesus. He chewed and swallowed a wedge of orange. "You have dreams, too, don't you, Danni?"*

*The girl looked into her bowl of salad, stabbed a radish, and lifted it to her mouth. She decided to treat the question as a rhetorical statement, but he persisted.*

*"I've seen the books you bring with you to work," said Jesus. "You're a generalist. You don't study just accounting and bookkeeping. You're into anthropology, sociology, psychology, criminology, and philosophy. You study people. I admire that. I truly do."*

*"I have a lot to learn," said Danielle.*

*"Yes, true enough," said Jesus, "but some people— and here I'm speaking from experience—are shown at a very young age that they've been gifted with rare abilities. Those abilities are instilled for a purpose. Let no one despise you for your youth, Danni. Instead, capitalize on your talents and use them in noble ways."*

*Danielle offered a small smile. "You sound like someone spouting lines from* <u>Great Expectations</u>.*"*

*"I think Freud could have benefited from reading more Dickens."*

43

*She liked that. She liked* <u>him</u>. *But then a sudden fear came over her, and before she could catch herself, for some reason she blurted, "Wait! You're not going to send me away, are you? Please, no. Have I failed in my work in some area?"*

*Jesus finished the last piece of orange and wiped his fingers on a napkin. "I'm planning on sending you away," admitted Jesus. "But not to get rid of you. To give you a chance to prove yourself. Plus, you'll be able to do something good for the company. It's time you were given your chance to show your worth."*

*"Where…where do I have to go?"*

*"Detroit."*

*"Who'll I be going with?"*

*"No one. You'll be on your own."*

*She narrowed her eyes. "This is company business? And I'll be going there alone? What is it you want me to do, sir?"*

*"The city fathers want to increase tourism in that area. Studies show that nostalgia has always been very big. Every year thousands of people go there to tour Henry Ford Museum and walk through Greenfield Village. So, they want to build an old-fashioned baseball park and hold exhibition games. The idea is to bring some of the big league stars out of retirement and also to invite teams from around the world. They'll let the fans go out on the field between games, and they'll arrange for autographs from the stars and sell some hotdogs, popcorn, and souvenirs. Just a lot of wholesome fun."*

*"I'm not a fan of hotdogs," said Danielle.*

*"I've heard that."*

*"What's our part in this?"*

*"Ten companies have been asked to come to a bidding showdown at the end of this month. The company that comes up with the best design, best ideas, and best sales pitch will land the contract to build a replica of a ballpark from more than a century ago. In those days the bleachers, superstructure, flagpoles, and dugouts were made entirely of wood. Our engineers and designers have submitted blueprints and bids. So have the other nine companies. The mayor is going to put the company reps together in a room for one day. He's going to grill them on why they think their designs and bids are the best options for the City of Detroit. Then, that day, one company will walk out of that room with a signed contract."*

*"Sounds intense," said Danielle.*

*"A regular den of lions," said Jesus.*

*"What's my part?"*

*"You're the one I'm throwing into the den."*

*She was silent a full moment. "Let me get this straight, sir..."*

*"You've already got it straight," said Jesus. "You've got two weeks to study the area where they're purposing to build the park...to get up to speed on our blueprints and bids...to learn all you can about the mayor of Detroit and his advisers —and to prepare your pitch."*

*"I'm…I'm nineteen. They'll eat me alive."*

*"Close their mouths," advised Jesus.*

*"Sir?"*

*"Go in prepared. Prepared to the teeth, if you'll pardon the pun. Whenever someone starts to attack what we're proposing, come back—roaring back, if you will—with precise reasons why their objections aren't applicable. Memorize statistics, compare costs, cite comparative studies. Do whatever you have to do, but don't let them devour you."*

*She imagined the scene for a moment—and it scared her. "But, they'll probably be mostly men," she said. "Their voices will be louder than mine. They'll be bigger than me. They'll be wearing thousand-dollar designer suits."*

*"Let their fires rage. Let their blustery winds roar. Then, when they're tired and spent, you can address them in a still, small voice. Offer reason and logic. Be the eye in the storm. If you have any fear, be still for a moment and know in your heart that I am with you."*

*Immediately, a genuine sense of contentment came over Danielle. She truly felt the presence of Jesus both beside her and within her. It made her smile.*

*"Yes, sir. I'll do my best," she said softly. Then, as an afterthought, she said, "Sir, before I go up there, can the company possibly spring for a pair of contact lenses?"*

*Jesus grinned. "Not a problem. I'm rather good at providing eye care."*

*The scene inside the bidding conclave wasn't exactly as Danielle had imagined it would be. Yes, there were eight men present, along with one other woman, each representing a longstanding and prestigious architectural firm. And, yes, they were dressed in power suits, and they had all the latest techno-gadgets at their disposal. But the leaders themselves didn't seem at the top of their game. In catching snatches of conversations here and there, Danielle could piece together that they had arrived several days ago. They'd spent their days schmoozing the local politicos and their evenings literally wining and dining members of the mayor's staff. As a result, several of them had bloodshot eyes, a few of the men wore their designer ties pulled away from the collars of their custom-made shirts, and one or two looked like they hadn't shaved in several days. Danielle, in contrast, had stuck to her diet of vegetables and water, had gotten adequate sleep, and was nicely groomed and neatly attired.*

*Mayor Henderson's chief of staff, a man named Ronald Roznowski, called for everyone to be seated around a large conference table. He and the mayor were at the head. Roznowski welcomed everyone and explained they'd each be given half an hour to make their presentations. However, before they began, the mayor had a challenge for them.*

*Henderson rose and clicked on an overhead projector. "Here on the project's website, you see a series of shots of the section of the city we plan to demolish and then renovate for the new stadium," the mayor began. He clicked through pictures of dilapidated buildings, garbage-strewn alleys, weed-infested lots, and abandoned schools. "This is what has me and my entire staff baffled, however. Since we announced our plans to revitalize this section of the city, these bizarre murals have been appearing on several of the buildings throughout the website."*

*The altered web photos showing area homes, apartment buildings, stores, and billboards each displayed an identical set of four clearly defined symbolic markings. "My people have no clue what this is all about, and since you people are experts on metropolitan renewal, I want you to tell me the meanings of these symbols. What does this strange writing mean?"*

*For a moment the room was silent, and then one man said, "Well, tell us who put them there, and we'll be able to tell you what they mean."*

*"You tell me," said the mayor. "If I knew who put them there, I'd go to that source directly."*

*"Well, then, tell us what you <u>think</u> they mean, Your Honor, and we'll let you know if we agree," said another man.*

*"I haven't got the slightest idea," said the mayor, growing testy. "Look, you're supposed to have all the answers. So, who among you can tell me the meaning of these symbols?"*

*The room was utterly soundless, all eyes looking down, no one making a sound, everyone desperately hoping that someone would come up with an answer so they could move on to the more serious nature of the meeting—the bidding war. Danielle realized that this was the eye-of-the-storm moment Jesus had said would come. He would expect her to make her move. But her heart was pounding, and her palms were sweating. She purposefully slowed her breathing, closed her eyes, and imagined the face of Jesus. She could see him smile and nod, and an immediate calmness came over her.*

*After what seemed an eternity, Danielle stood at the end of the table. In a low but clear voice, she said, "I can interpret the meaning of the symbols, Your Honor."*

*The mayor squinted down the table at the young woman, then turned to Roznowski and raised an eyebrow. Quickly, Roznowski flipped through some papers and whispered, "Danielle Beltzer, Tree of Life Furnishings.*

*"Yes…Ms. Beltzer? You have some insight on this, do you?" asked Henderson.*

*"It's called urban guerilla tagging, sir. In this case, the photos are tagged instead of the structures themselves. And part of the message is for you, personally."*

*The others around the table began to stir again, some smirking, some even chuckling slightly. But the mayor did not dismiss the young woman's comments. "Please," he said, "continue."*

*Danielle pointed to the first image. "What you see, sir, is a huge hand with an open palm facing forward, and across the palm is a large X. This symbol means all outsiders are to stop in their tracks and not enter this territory. It's a warning from local gangs that outsiders will be considered trespassers."*

*Now everyone was paying attention to the screen. Danielle continued. "The second symbol is a large round sun with beaming rays streaming from it, while below it is a crescent moon surrounded by stars. This is a warning that whether day or night, the gangs will be on patrol and ready to defend their turf. They will be vigilant, prepared, coiled in a striking position."*

*Danielle slowly walked along the side of the table, closer to the screen. "The third image shows a large, muscular fist. Around it are six identical fists forming a circle of unity. This symbol means all six gangs controlling that section of Detroit have formed a temporary alliance. They're now working as one, huge, well-armed gang. If your wrecking crews enter any section of their territory, all of the gangs will move in on that section and will commence all-out war until your workers are driven off."*

*As she reached the front of the room, Danielle lowered her voice even more. She looked directly at the mayor and said, "This fourth and final symbol is a personal warning, Your Honor. You see the crude outline of a home with what seem to be flames coming from it. Below it is a target with a letter*

*H stenciled on the bull's eye and lightning-bolt arrows flying in from all sides. This symbol means that if you authorize the destruction of their homes for this new project, they are going to send a death squad for you and your family. It will become a personal vendetta, and even if your project gets built, those sending this message will ultimately see to it that you, your wife, and your children are killed."*

*The mayor's face went ashen. After a few seconds someone from the far end of the table started saying, "What a bunch of hogwash. Who does she…?" but the mayor yelled, "Silence!" No one said another word.*

*"How? How do you know these things?" asked the mayor, his full attention on Danielle.*

*"My boss," she began, "says you have to understand people, not just know business principles. I study cultures, sir. I study people. What you are doing here is threatening the only way of life these folks have ever known. If you take away their streets and dwellings and local shops, they'll have no place to go. To them, it's death either way. So, they might as well go down fighting and at least have their dignity."*

*"But can there be no compromise?" asked the mayor.*

*"Of course there can," Danielle assured him. She inhaled a deep breath and took a moment to collect her thoughts. Forcing herself to stay confident enough to finish her assignment, she said, "But you have to meet with them. Speak*

*their language. Discuss terms they can relate to. Offer options that provide them with some hope and optimism."*

*The mayor looked down the table at the useless gathering of supposed expert analysts. "These people are of no help to me in this," he said. Turning back to Danielle he said, "What about you? Will you join my staff, lead this revitalization project, help me negotiate terms with the people in these neighborhoods? I'll give you anything you could want. We can come up with a job title for you, a good salary, outstanding benefits."*

*Danielle suddenly felt that inner presence of Jesus come over her stronger than ever, as if to indicate she had accomplished what he'd sent her to do. She smiled benignly. "I don't want the special perks, Your Honor, but I'll be glad to help you."*

*"Name your price," he said. "Tell me what you do want. It's yours."*

*Almost shyly, Danielle said, "It would be nice to go back with that contract for the new development project."*

*"Done," said the mayor, waving at Roznowski to assemble the paperwork. "Excellent! I can see this is going to be very beneficial." He paused then added, "Hey, I have an idea. Since we've finished early today, why don't you stay over another night? I have a private box at the stadium, and you could attend the football game with us tomorrow. Detroit is at home this weekend. How about it?"*

*"The Lions?" said Danielle. "Thanks . . . but no."*

# THE SECRET OF SERENDIPITY: LUCK IS A MYTH

People who believe in luck are their own worst enemies. Napoleon Bonaparte once said derisively, "Yes, I believe in luck. I believe in *bad* luck, and I believe that I will have it. Therefore, I plan accordingly."

Hundreds of thousands of people go to casinos each year hoping to hit it big. The casinos, wanting to perpetuate the notion that people can get something for nothing, arrange for there to be a big winner once or twice each day.

To the outside observer, it looks as though someone has bet $100 and walked away with $10,000. But where did the casino get all the cash to buy the land, build elaborate gaming rooms, pay for machines and card and dice tables, hire waitresses and dealers, pay for flashing lights and air conditioning, and provide all the free beverages being handed out to patrons? Those funds came from the thousands of people who bet $100 and walked away with nothing. The odds are always with the house.

All gambling systems work in similar fashion. There are far more losers than winners. But even winning big doesn't guarantee happiness. Statistics show that very often the people who hit state lotteries wind up leading miserable lives. One woman's children were kidnapped and held for ransom. One man was bombarded by long-lost relatives coming to ask for handouts. Another fellow didn't understand his legal liabilities, went on a spending spree, and wound up losing everything he'd purchased when the IRS foreclosed on him for unpaid taxes.

As often as not, people who are "lucky" enough to inherit a fortune or win the lottery or receive a large lawsuit settlement or hit the right number at the casino sooner or later wind up right back as poor as they were when they started—or even worse off.

## Sweat Equity

I've heard marvelously ironic statements when people talk about luck. One guy said, "Yeah, my great-great-grandfather went west during the 1847 gold rush. He worked for fourteen years staking claims and working mines, and finally he got *lucky* and hit a pocket vein and came away with more than fifty thousand bucks."

The guy labored like a dog for fourteen years before finding gold? You call that *lucky*?

Similarly, I heard my wife's aunt say many years ago, "After the Depression, my husband Phil got into the car business. He struggled for a long time, usually having only eight or ten cars to sell on our lot and only one garage for repairs. But, *lucky* for us, times got better and eventually we owned two huge dealerships and numerous garages."

Her husband struggled to make ends meet for more than a decade, building his business, conserving his money, establishing his reputation, steadily expanding his operation, and his wife thought that one day they just got *lucky?* Luck had nothing to do with it. Phil, himself, told me that his success came from sweat equity. He put in endless hours, leveraged his cash, met the needs of his customers, and one day reached his goal of finding great success as the owner of two car dealerships.

Luck, whether good or bad, usually is nothing more than the result of what physicists refer to as "cause and effect." What you initiate determines what chain of events you set off and what results you get. The Bible explains it as, "Whatever you sow, you reap." Plant corn and you'll reap corn. Plant love in your youngsters and you'll reap grown children who will care for you in your old age. Conversely, negative behavior will reap negative outcomes. It really is that simple.

You've heard it said that even a blind squirrel finds a nut now and then. That's not true. Blind squirrels get eaten by wolves. You've also heard about the "luck of the draw," but what that actually refers to is a mathematical probability factor, not luck. Weather forecasters, sports-games odds makers, and stock market analysts use such probability factors all the time. These women and men are not guessing or hoping; they are estimating and calculating. You've heard terms like "fool luck," "dumb luck," "blind luck," "random luck," and "beginner's luck." The reason there are so many stabs at trying to give a name to luck is because luck doesn't exist and, as such, it is neither identifiable nor quantifiable.

But, does this mean that great opportunities never arise? Does it mean that phenomenal quantum leaps cannot be taken at unexpected junctures in life? No, not at all. In fact, what might be labeled as "a fair shake" or "a unique situation" or "a sudden opening" or "the chance of a lifetime" or "my one big shot at success" is far more the norm than most people realize. Golden moments present themselves at regular intervals, but only those people who can recognize them, capitalize on them, and "reap" their benefits will understand that they are not "lucky," they are *prepared*.

## Serendipity

One of the great debates related to "cause and effect" concerns how much of cause and effect is instigated by serendipitous circumstances. In other words, if an opportunity to advance oneself arises seemingly by happenstance, and one decides to take advantage of this opportunity, does the credit go to fool luck for having made the opportunity available, or does it go to the decisive individual who recognized the opportunity and grabbed it? To answer this, let's examine a centuries-old statement: "When the student is ready, the teacher will appear."

The implication of this statement is, if a person is curious, open, and ready to learn, this eagerness alone will cause a teacher to manifest himself or herself. But that, of course, is stupid. A corollary would have to be, "When the poor person is ready to become wealthy, strongboxes of gold will be shipped to him." One statement is as ridiculous as the other.

What actually happens is far more logical. If I, in my role as college professor, discover a highly motivated student with talents and abilities, I will pour myself into that student, knowing that my investment will not be wasted. As a teacher, I can see that the student is ready, so I will step in with guidance. Similarly, if a student is motivated enough to want to learn a subject, he or she will *seek* a teacher, and, fortunately, teachers are not hard to find. Professors, mentors, librarians, co-workers, seminar leaders, advisers, authors, and workshop instructors are readily accessible. Any student of any subject can find a teacher. The process has nothing to do with luck or good fortune or being at the right place at the right time. It is all cause and effect: The student needs a teacher, so he or she finds a teacher.

This leads us, however, to another question. More than just recognizing opportunities worth pursuing as they arise, can the success-oriented individual purposefully open more doors for advancement? Phrased another way, can people *make their own luck*? For a fact, this actually can be done, and it is less difficult than one might think. Here are some ways to go about it.

***See your circumstances in a broader spectrum.*** Too often our tunnel vision related to our talents and assignments and specific businesses will limit us to minimal opportunities. When Lee Iacocca took over the financially crippled Chrysler Corporation, he changed the company's perspective about its upside potential. He explained that they were not in the business of producing vehicle models such as the New Yorker or Imperial or LeBaron. They were in the "transportation" business. They needed to discover how America wanted to be "transported" and then deliver those products. This led to the development of the minivan, which made Chrysler millions of dollars in profit, as well as the K-cars, which were years ahead of their time in fuel efficiency and compact styling. However, it also led

Chrysler to buy the Gulfstream Aerospace Corporation, because that purchase aligned with the new mission of being in the overall "transportation business."

Expand your horizons in a similar fashion. You're not just a high school speech teacher, you are a professional communicator. This means you can also do consulting work as a corporate speech coach, earn extra money by creating a school debate team, and begin to get paid to deliver motivational speeches at clubs and conventions. Likewise, you're not just a groundskeeper, you are an agricultural architect. Use your experience to offer services in home landscaping, outdoor party decorating, and in "going green" in new office buildings. Give yourself a bigger title, a grander spectrum of challenges, and a wider array of new vistas.

**Explore tandem ventures.** Many times just by looking at our circumstances from a new perspective, we can launch into unusual but scintillating avenues of progress. For example: Is that an upset apple cart, or is it the invention of applesauce? Is that a pile of sooty broken glass, or is it the invention of sunglasses?

When I needed to move in a hurry from Muncie to North Manchester, Indiana, so that I could accept a good job offer to become a public relations director at the local college, I was in a panic about selling my home in

Muncie. My dad suggested that I take a different approach. "Why not ask the college if it has any temporary housing available? If it does, take it, and make this home of yours in Muncie a rental property. Your tenants can then pay off your mortgage for you."

It turned out that for a low monthly fee I would be able to rent a house in North Manchester within walking distance from my job. I signed a lease, then got renters for my home in Muncie, and, suddenly, I was in the real estate business. I've been the owner of rental properties ever since, adding houses in other cities throughout the years. It was a great business opportunity for me, but I would have missed it if my father hadn't made me look at a tandem concept, i.e. instead of selling a home, consider renting out a home.

***Attempt cross-pollination of ideas.*** Nature does not create all of the delicious fruit varieties we enjoy. Humans have been able to cross-pollinate various seeds to develop new creations. A plumcot, for instance, is a cross between a plum and an apricot. A tangelo is a cross between a tangerine and a grapefruit. This same sort of experimentation can be done in art, business, sports, finance, education, or architecture.

In 1971 a woman who taught sales workshops won a Caribbean cruise from her company when she helped the sales staff exceed a million dollars in revenue. While out in the middle of the sea, it dawned on the trainer that cruise ships would be fantastic places to hold seminars and workshops. The participants would love the environment and could deduct the expense of the trip as a business investment, and the hosting organization would have a better turnout and, thus, earn more registration income. The trainer contacted the cruise line and asked for special seminar rooms and discount prices if she could guarantee seventy-five participants for a future "seminar at sea." The cruise line saw this as a great way to book more passengers, so it readily agreed. This combination became a win-win-win situation: the trainer drew a larger crowd, the cruise ship booked more passengers, and the passengers got tax deductions because part of their cruise involved a business training seminar. The concept opened the door to what is now a big aspect of cruise ship bookings. The trainer never would have thought of this great new concept if she had not left the office and gone to a totally new locale.

Mixing and blending seemingly divergent entities can result in fantastic innovations. Take away the ice skates and the horses and combine hockey with polo, and you get field hockey. Combine a general store with a gas station and you get a modern "Gas and Go" or mini-mart. Combine a pick-up truck, a van, and a station wagon, and you get a mini-van. Start with a TV screen, add a typewriter and a memory chip, and you get a word processor. Mix a computer with a pinball machine and you get a video game.

Former TV personality Art Linkletter once told an audience that when he was a kid the little boys would run alongside a hoop, keeping it upright and balanced with a stick. The little girls would play on the merry-go-round, swirling their bodies to keep the momentum going. Turning the hoop sideways and keeping it going by emulating the act of swirling the merry-go-round resulted in the hula-hoop. Linkletter invested in the product and made a fortune.

To cross pollinate ideas and concepts, you will need to go where you have not gone before, either physically or mentally. Develop new hobbies (collecting coins, dolls, or figurines; shooting pool; rebuilding cars). Travel to new locales (tropical islands, barren deserts, mountain ridges). Read books outside of your normal area of interest (mysteries, romances, westerns, comedies). Talk to folks in all walks of life (beauticians, bankers, babysitters, birdwatchers, baristas). Keep a notepad handy. Thoughts that are stimulated in new regions of your mind will need to be recorded, processed, and applied.

**Avoid being an "also ran."** If you want to be original, don't run with the pack. The trend is to jump on a bandwagon and join the merriment. However, it usually turns out to be a different metaphor: a ship that has already sailed. Admittedly, sometimes you have to match your competition, as in the case when Chrysler made so much money from minivans,that the other carmakers had to start producing them, too. But, usually, once someone breaks out with a new idea, anything that comes after it will be a watered down version of the original. One need only compare a movie like *Battleship Earth* to the original *Star Wars* to see how bad the imitations and copycats can be.

***Canvass your clientele.*** Many times breakthrough strategies and ideas can come from those you serve. Surveys, questionnaires, focus group meetings, and evaluation cards are useful in seeing your operation from the customer's perspective. For example, the idea of building elevators on the *outside* of hotel buildings to save indoor space actually came from someone who was not a hotel employee.

Similarly, a government employee at the start of the Civil War was challenged by President Lincoln to find a fast way to get news from one coast to the other while the transcontinental telegraph was still being established. The man couldn't think of an answer, but he happened to mention this problem one night to his family at dinner. His young son, who ran relay races in high school, suggested a "horse relay." The father was astounded at the simplicity of the notion, and by April 1860, the Pony Express was running mail every ten days from St. Joseph, Missouri, to Sacramento, California, a distance of more than 1,950 miles. It stayed in operation until October 1861, when the telegraph link-up was completed. (Out of the mouths of babes, eh?)

## Luck Isn't Part of the Equation

One important factor about serendipity is that coming up with a clever idea and carrying it out are two different matters. When Fred Smith looked at a fuse box and saw how all the wires came into one central distribution point and then sent power back out in new directions, it gave him the idea of using Memphis, Tennessee, as a central gathering place for airplanes carrying mail. It was a great idea, but had he never acted on this breakthrough concept and created Federal Express, the idea would have been of no use to him or to his future customers. Smith wasn't "lucky" in creating Federal Express; he was intelligent, focused, disciplined, goal-oriented, and determined.

If you've been waiting for your "lucky break," it's time to face the fact that it will never happen. Luck is a myth; however, thinking and speculating and dreaming—and then putting plans together to make your dreams become reality—is something real. Pay attention to innovative thoughts. In fact, use the processes in this section to stimulate such thoughts. In doing so, you'll discover the wisdom of the adage, "The harder I work, the luckier I get."

## Key Points Found in Section *3*

1. Luck is a myth.

2. Luck, whether good or bad, is nothing more than the result of cause and effect. What you initiate determines what chain of events you set off and what results you get.

3. Golden moments present themselves at regular intervals, but only those people who recognize them and reap their benefits will realize they weren't lucky; they were prepared.

4. See your circumstances in a broader spectrum. Give yourself a bigger title and a grander array of new vistas.

5. Explore tandem ventures. By looking at your circumstances from a new perspective, you can launch into avenues of progress.

6. Attempt cross-pollination of ideas. Mixing and blending seemingly divergent entities can result in fantastic innovations.

7. Avoid being an "also ran." Avoid running with the pack.

8. Canvass your clientele. Many times breakthrough strategies and ideas can come from those you serve.

9. Coming up with a clever idea and carrying it out are two different matters.

*"I specifically told you to go forth and tell no man."*

*"And I blatantly disobeyed you," said Matt Feingold, flashing a wide, toothy grin. "I not only told all men, I also told all women. So, today's your birthday, and everyone in the plant wants to help you celebrate. Cake and ice cream await you in the main assembly room."*

*"But what was the reason for putting it online?"*

*"You have a strong social networking base: 'What a <u>friend</u> we have in Jesus.' I know you've heard it."*

*Jesus grimaced. "Beware when all men speak well of you."*

*Matt moved to the office door. "You and your bromides. Come on. Turning thirty-three won't kill you."*

*Jesus raised an eyebrow but gave no response.*

*As they passed through the outer office, Martha rose from behind her desk. "You're getting mountains of e-mails, letters, and cards today, Boss, but the weirdest thing has been the arrival a few minutes ago of these little crates. They were hand delivered by a small delegation from the U.N. The delegation is in the lobby, right now, wanting to see you, if possible. Three men, ambassadors from Middle Eastern countries where we've set up overseas assembly plants this past year."*

*"You're serious?" said Matt. "Three U.N. Ambassadors are <u>here</u>, right now, in our lobby? No way."*

"*They're legit all right. They gave me their cards, and I did a web search. You wouldn't believe the schools these guys attended and the degrees they've earned. Talk about three smart guys—wow!*"

"*So, what's in the crates?*" asked Matt.

Jesus glanced over and said, "*A gold medallion, an urn of frankincense, and a clay jar of myrrh.*"

"*I'm not going to ask you how you know that already,*" said Matt, "*and I'm still going to keep lobbying for us to get a bomb-sniffing dog or at least some X-ray machines to use on all the shipments we get in here.*"

"*I'll let you know when danger arrives,*" said Jesus.

"*Uh, what's myrrh?*" asked Martha.

"*It's a rather expensive and somewhat rare clove mixture,*" said Matt. "*They use it in the East primarily in the preparation of corpses.*"

Martha flinched. "*My word! What kind of a warped person would give burial spices as a birthday present?*"

Jesus looked at the small crate. "*My assumption would be, someone who was a very wise man and could see into the future.*"

"*So, how do we want to handle this?*" asked Matt.

Jesus said, "*Show the three ambassadors into my office. You two go get the party started. I'll be along in a half hour or so. I need to listen to what these men want to share with me.*"

*"Okay," said Matt, "but we're also having pizza, so don't be late."*

*This amused Jesus. "When you're on your own time schedule, you're never late."*

*Half an hour later, city employee Miguel Gomez was sweeping the sidewalk when he saw Jesus and three men in Middle-Eastern garb approach a stretch limo at the curb. Each visitor bowed to Jesus and addressed him in sincere deference before climbing into the vehicle.*

*As the limousine pulled away, Jesus turned and called, "Miguel Gomez, come to me."*

*Startled, the sidewalk sweeper fought rising panic. Who was this man? A Fed with* <u>La Migra</u>? *Would he demand to see Miguel's papers? It wouldn't be the first time Miguel had been singled out because of his ethnicity.* <u>Just play it cool, muchacho,</u> *he told himself, taking a deep breath. "You—you know my name, Señor?"*

*"Of course. You are a dear friend of mine," said Jesus. "I am greatly indebted to you."*

*Miguel looked over his shoulder to determine if someone else might be the one being addressed. Well, maybe the man wasn't a Fed, but obviously he was a little* <u>loco</u>. *Miguel looked at Jesus and pointed at himself questioningly. "You no can mean me, Señor. Never have we met. I...I have done you no favors."*

*"Don't be modest, Miguel. You fed me when I was hungry. You gave me something to drink when I was thirsty. You clothed me when I was cold."*

*Miguel squinted. No...no, he was quite sure he had never met this man. And now that he thought about it, surely a man to whom others bowed would not be someone who would be drunk or insane. This was very confusing. "Perdón Señor, but when do you think I gave you a meal?"*

*"Not more than a week ago," said Jesus. "Right here on this sidewalk."*

*Very slowly Miguel leaned his broom against the building wall. He edged closer to Jesus, studying the man's face with close scrutiny. He discerned no guile, no mockery, no deception. "Lo siento, but I do not remember this."*

*"Last Tuesday morning," Jesus explained. "You were here sweeping this walkway. A man arrived with a little boy. It was seven o'clock, but the man wanted to be first in line when we opened the door at nine so that he could apply for a job. They were poorly dressed, it was chilly, and you heard the little boy say he was hungry. They'd had no supper nor any breakfast."*

*Miguel's eyes widened. Yes, he remembered that day, but how did this stranger know about these people? And what did their circumstances matter to him?*

70

*"You went down the street and bought a bag of doughnuts and two paper cups of hot chocolate and came back and gave them to the man and his son. You took off your jacket and put it around the boy's shoulders."*

For a moment Miguel was amazed that the man could know all this. He looked left and right, in front of him and in back, down and up. And then he spotted it. A security camera was mounted high on the ledge of the building. *"Oh,"* he said to himself, then louder, *"you have the eye in the sky."*

Jesus enjoyed the irony. *"Indeed, I do, Miguel, indeed, I do."*

*"<u>Sí</u>. You gave the man a job? Yes? No?"*

*"I gave him a job, yes. He's now one of my people, Miguel. And whenever anyone does something good for my people, I consider it doing good for me."*

Miguel lowered his eyes. *"It was so little. <u>De nada, Señor</u>."*

*"It wasn't <u>nothing</u> from my perspective."* Jesus pointed to an entryway. *"There's a bit of a banquet going on inside there right now. It's in my honor. Today is my birthday. I'm going to walk you in and seat you beside me as the other guest of honor."*

Miguel looked utterly bewildered and even a bit scared. *"<u>Excúsame, Señor</u>. I am a stranger to these people. <u>Yo</u>—guest of honor, at <u>your</u> banquet? <u>Es imposible</u>."*

*"I've called ahead and prepared a place for you. Where I am, you will be also. I know your deeds, and I am well*

*pleased." He pointed again toward the door. "Enter into your reward." Jesus put a hand on Miguel's shoulder and gently nudged him ahead.*

*Together, they opened the door. Immediately, as Miguel stepped forward, a large crowd began to sing, "For he's the jolly,* <u>good</u> *fellow!"*

# Section *4*

# The Slow-but-Steady Shift

Visual images in nature can be deceptive. Volcanic eruptions appear as sudden, unstoppable explosions. Lava spews hundreds of feet into the air and then rolls in thick rivers of fire down the mountainside. Smoke belches in dense, massive waves of darkness. Steam hisses like a locomotive. The ground rumbles and shakes. Temperatures rise to intolerable levels. The planet, so it *seems*, has suddenly blown a gasket.

But, this simply is not true. In reality, plate-tectonic flexes have been occurring below the earth's surface for centuries. Rock shifts have opened gorges, pushed forth lava, sent steam into pockets, and altered balances of sand and soil and water. The earth has been coiling, expanding, bending, bulging, caving in, rising up, and repositioning itself in slow but never-ending maneuvers. Finally, immense buildups of power and force and compressed energy exploit a weak spot in the earth's crust and rush all of their compressed might into that one channel, causing an eruption of pulverized and melted rock to explode into freedom. From deep down, numerous layers of molten rock are uniting to produce weeks and even months of fireworks, flame, light, and instability.

This works as a metaphor for artists, writers, dancers, inventors, scientists, and athletes who seem to have a sudden "breakthrough moment" that thrusts them into the international limelight. Unwittingly, observers will quip, "I wish I could be an overnight success like that person." For a fact, within those successful individuals, life-tectonic flexes have been at work for many years, ultimately resulting in the bursting-forth of success. Their schooling, jobs, moves, failures, disappointments, travels, and achievements have been shaping these individuals below the surface. Their families, friends, neighbors, pastors, teachers, mentors, and coaches have flexed them in many ways. The books they've read, movies they've watched, goals they've set, births and deaths they've witnessed, and projects they've been involved in have bent, bulged, and blossomed them into the rising spectacles they have become. They are getting out of life what they have put into it. This is another way that the "sweat equity" concept we talked about earlier leads to personal success.

## Dormant Volcanoes

No matter where you may be in life right now, if you are a person of goals and dreams, you may be asking, "Lord, if I am so willing, eager, and ready, why does time keep slipping by without my experiencing a volcanic eruption of success?"

Trust me, I can identify with that feeling of inner frustration. When I was eighteen and had just finished high school, I was gung-ho about entering the world of professional writing. My high school English teachers had told me I was a gifted writer, and two of my short stories had been published in the school's literary magazine during my senior year. I was ready to see my name in print, to experience success in the literary world, and to earn a good income as a writer.

But it didn't happen. At least, not then. In fact, it was a full decade before I experienced what could be called significant success as a writer. And it wasn't because I hadn't been trying. I had gone to college and earned AA, BA, and MA degrees in English, and then I'd started working on a PhD in literature and linguistics. And I'd been reading mountains of books about aspects of writing, not to mention reading, cover to cover, the various monthly writers' magazines I subscribed to. Oh, and my effort to crack into national magazines was tireless, if ever heartbreaking. The stack of rejection letters—most of them form replies—could have served as wallpaper for my little home office. The only reason I continued to pursue a career in writing was because every now and then an editor would throw me a bone, such as the sale of a filler to a regional publication or perhaps a little story to a Sunday school take-home paper, which, I should add, paid half a penny a word back in the 1970s.

But then, indeed, in time, the volcano burst forth. In 1982 I wrote a book called *Positive Workaholism* that took off like a rocket. It wasn't a lengthy book, and the publisher wasn't well-known. It was released by R & R Newkirk, which was the business imprint of the now-defunct Bobbs-Merrill Publishing Company. Nevertheless, the book clicked with readers, first those in business and later the general public. It went through several printings. Excerpts from it were published in national magazines. I was hired to write an audio script of the book that became an extremely successful book on tape for Success Motivation Institute. I was invited on radio and TV talk shows and featured in newspapers and magazines. Offers came pouring in for speaking engagements and to write more books. And, on top of all that, I completed my PhD in May of that year.

So, here I was, after ten years of struggling, limping along, coping with very limited success, suddenly both a doctor of literature and linguistics and the author of a best-selling book. And, believe it or not, at my first couple of autograph parties, at least a dozen people said to me, "I wish I could be lucky like you and write a hit book." That drove me nuts. *Lucky?* I wanted to scream, "I spent nine years in college earning that doctor's degree! I invested ten years of my life practicing the craft of writing. Luck had nothing to do with it. It was sweat equity." But I held my tongue because I could see in the eyes of each of those people a mystical dream of wanting to "make it," and to make it *soon.* And I knew they all were questioning why time was slipping by, relentlessly aging them without rewarding them for hoping and longing and desiring. And I also held my tongue because I felt sorry for most of them. They had the dreams and yearnings for success; they just didn't have the gumption needed to log the time and exert the effort required to reach that success.

## No Instantaneous Rewards

Among the many lessons we can learn from the Bible is this one: Success at anything comes slowly. Noah and his sons spent decades building the ark. Joshua spent forty years as the assistant to Moses before he was elevated to a leadership position. Elisha served many years under the tutelage of Elijah. Samuel served under Eli. Esther had to undergo a year of preparation under the care of Hegai before she had her chance to become queen. Jesus, himself, waited thirty years before initiating his preaching and teaching and healing ministry. The disciples trained for three years under Jesus before being sent out on their own.

Was there a logic in this, a rationale for such long delays? I don't have all the answers, but I can make some observations. Noah and his sons served as proclaimers of the pending judgment God planned to bring upon the world. No one who watched them work or who listened to their reasons for building the ark could say he or she did not have adequate warning. Joshua did spend a long time serving under Moses, but then God allowed Joshua to live an extremely long life, thus compensating for any invested youthful years as an underling. Elisha was subservient to Elijah, but, ultimately, in his own right, he was a great prophet and performed many miracles. Samuel knew even as a youngster what his life calling was, but that did not negate his need to train for it. Understanding of his calling only set him on the precise course for his life's mission. Esther was equipped with natural beauty and a reverent spirit toward God and authority, but she needed to learn all aspects of how the royal court worked in order to function at peak performance when called upon to save her people. The disciples spent three years observing Jesus in action, listening to his teachings, asking questions, making mistakes and realigning judgments, failing but learning, and equipping themselves to be teachers on their own in time. Success is never automatic, even in the service of God. It requires training, patience, and grit.

## Three Important Lessons

Considering those who have achieved a level of success—whether in biblical times or more recently—I believe there are three lessons we can glean from their experiences.

***It does no good to dwell on past failures and false starts.*** The corollary to "nothing ventured, nothing gained" is "nothing ventured, nothing lost." Indeed, if we make a serious stab at succeeding at something, we run the risk of failing miserably. And if that happens, we can wind up embarrassed and disappointed. It can cause us to hesitate trying other endeavors. As the saying goes, once burned, twice shy.

But, here again, if we study successful people in the Bible, we will quickly see a line-up of folks who often began as colossal failures. For example, Jonah did evangelize the entire city of Nineveh, but that was after he had run from his assignment and had been in the belly of the great fish for three days as punishment. And, yes, John Mark did write one of the Gospels, and he did serve Paul when Paul was in prison, but that was after Paul had "fired" John Mark for his lackluster performance on the original missionary journey undertaken by Paul and Barnabas. And, indeed, Peter did preach before thousands, and he did perform miracles in the name of Christ, but that was after denying three times that he was associated with or even knew Jesus.

The legacy of failures among leaders (King Saul, King David, King Solomon…the list seems endless) is well documented and known by even casual students of the Scriptures. The more important point is that many of these successful people used their errors and mistakes as life lessons, made adjustments and improvements, and came back stronger than ever. So can you.

If you've ever looked at the glowing projections of future earnings outlined in a mutual fund or stock portfolio prospectus, you've see colorful charts and bar graphs rising higher and higher on the earnings scales. However, at the very bottom of the page in microscopic print you will find the line, "Past performance is no guarantee of future success." Brokers must insert that line because history has shown that no one can predict with total accuracy the rise and fall of the stock market. Salespeople need an escape clause should you ever come back and wonder why all your investment money has suddenly disappeared.

A paraphrase of that statement, "Past performance is no guarantee of future failure," is applicable to developing leaders and people seeking success in their careers. Just because you may have bottomed out in one endeavor is no reason to feel you cannot succeed at something different. As Paul recommended, forget what is behind and strive toward what is ahead (Philippians 3:13). Don't let one bad incident thwart you from starting afresh on something equally as exciting and challenging.

***Don't look down at your feet when you are walking on water.*** When you invest time and energy, you will almost always begin to experience success at reaching your goals. However, that is not a time to gloat, brag, pause, or rest on your merits. Similarly, it is not a time to have second thoughts about your noble ambitions, to question the validity of your achievements, or to doubt your personal capabilities. When Peter charged out of the boat and went striding on the water toward Christ, he was walking by faith. But, when he looked down and began to assess the normality of the scene he was in, his faith waned and he began to sink. His mistake was in taking his eyes off his goal. You dare not make a similar error. Stay focused.

I have been the keynote speaker at conferences and conventions attended by thousands of entrepreneurs, business owners, franchisees, and start-up wannabes. During the convention, I've seen the attendees become enthused by motivational speakers, workshop leaders, and seminar presenters. The folks in the audience begin to believe that, yes, they can return home, expand their advertising efforts, train their employees to be more efficient, expand their product offerings, and dress up their store appeal. With all this new knowledge, success is a sure thing.

However, follow-up research shows that most of these novice executives will lose that enthusiasm once they return to Villeville, USA, and realize it will take more than a couple of rah-rah speeches and some vague promises of a Christmas bonus or a better sales commission to get the home team as fired up about major advances as the boss is. Consequently, the boss/owner/supervisor/manager takes his or her eyes off the vision and begins to sink.

Let that be a lesson, even an admonition. You must neither take your eyes off your goal nor stop striving toward it. If yours is not a solo endeavor, it will be all the more imperative that others see you are never wavering in your forward momentum. They will take their cue from you, their leader and role model. So, be buoyed by your enthusiasm, confidence, and worthy ambitions. Don't look down at the water; stay focused on the quest.

***Plant your ideas and nurture your dreams.*** I noted earlier that people who want overnight success have no concept of what it takes to reach the top in any endeavor. You have to start small and grow as you go. Not everything will pan out, but some things will. You have to capitalize on the winning efforts and abandon the losing ventures.

Jesus gave a good example of this when he told the story of the person who sowed seeds. He said some seeds fell on rocky ground, and recouping the cost of those seeds proved to be hopeless. Other seeds fell on poor soil, and even though the seeds germinated, their roots were so sparse, they withered and died. Fortunately, a substantial amount of seed fell on rich soil, and those seeds became numerous strong, flourishing plants that eventually produced a bumper crop.

I can liken this to my fledgling career as a writer. Many, many of my early manuscripts fell on rocky soil. They were rejected because I sent the material to the wrong markets, I didn't use the correct manuscript format, or my writing wasn't yet polished enough to "take root" with the publications I approached. Other manuscripts fell on poor soil. Yes, they were accepted and published, but the pay scale was so abysmal, and the byline exposure was so limited, those bits of success did very little to advance my career as a budding author. However, in time, still other manuscripts found rich soil and were given vast distribution and more substantial monetary compensations.

Your career path will follow a similar pattern—some total failures, some modest successes, and some huge breakthroughs. But nothing will happen if you don't initiate the process. You have to plant your ideas, then you must nurture the seedlings of progress by continuing to learn and develop and hone your skills and knowledge. Finally, after months and years of planting and nurturing, you can harvest the bumper crop and use your well-earned success to enjoy your dream while providing benefit to others.

## Lessons from Nature

We observed earlier that it takes centuries before a volcano is ready to erupt. Nature presents that same lesson in myriad ways. A massive oak may begin as an acorn, but a hundred years later it will have transformed into a tree whose long, thick branches now can reach to the sky and are supported by a massive trunk. A little stream may break away from a rolling river and form a trickle into a valley, but with a hundred years of drainage, it can carve a new riverbed and create a mighty tributary. A light snowfall may continue to add layer upon layer to a mountainside until eventually the mass is so enormous, it crushes beneath its own weight and sends an avalanche of tons of snow barreling down the mountain, obliterating anything in its path.

Mighty works come with time, persistence, and consistent effort. Each miniscule part may not seem significant by itself (one melted rock? one acorn starting to germinate? one snowflake resting on the side of a massive mountain?), yet collectively the elements create momentum, add bulk, and increase stability.

So, take a lesson from nature. It's never too late to start. The secret is realizing that while overnight successes don't exist, a slow and steady pace will ultimately pay off.

## Key Points Found in Section *4*

1. There are no overnight success stories. Success comes with time and effort.

2. Nature shows that slow, steady progress results in major achievements.

3. Even heroes in Bible times had to spend years being mentored and trained before they rose to levels of leadership and success.

4. Past failures are no indication that future failures are inevitable.

5. Some efforts will fail, some will be modest successes, and some will lead to major breakthroughs.

6. Once success starts to arrive, don't be arrogant about it, and don't start second-guessing yourself.

7. If your success is dependent on a team effort, exude the confidence and vision needed to inspire those around you.

*This was the third summer company picnic Judas had to endure, and each one seemed worse than its predecessor. Taking a whole day off just to sit around talking, eating snacks, and playing games when there was so much work the employees could be doing riled Judas no end. He was determined he would locate Jesus, wherever he was mingling with the masses today, and get his signature on some contracts and his authorization for some new mergers.*

*Dressed in his standard three-piece suit, Judas wove his way through the covey of families and their friends. He could not help but catch snatches of the stories being shared.*

*Jonah Atwater was saying, "So, I told the Boss there was no way I was going to San Francisco to represent the company. Big cities scare the daylights out of me. But the Boss kept saying, no, this was my responsibility, and I needed to face up to it. But I told him, nothing in the world could be worse than having to board a plane for San Francisco. Boy, was I wrong about that! On Friday evening, just before a three-day holiday weekend, I went down to our walk-in vault to secure the day's deposits and payments. I was putting everything in order, when suddenly the vault door closed behind me and sealed itself."*

*Atwater's eyes bulged as he tried to recreate his sense of horror for the audience seated around him at the picnic table. "I ran to the door and tried to open it, but the tumblers were preset to stay locked until Tuesday morning at 9:00. I pounded on the door and screamed, but, of course, it was soundproof. There I was, locked in the belly of that vault for three days and three nights, and all I had was a roll of LifeSavers in my pocket. My cell phone couldn't work inside the vault. I spent those three days saying over and over to myself, 'Why didn't I go to San Francisco as I was supposed to?' I wondered if I'd even survive, and as each hour passed...."*

*Judas moved on. Standing next to a different picnic table, he scanned the horizon. Gideon Marshall was rambling on about his five months in South America. "But when the Boss signaled for me to come off the line to talk to him, I thought he just wanted to show me some new blueprints. Instead, he tells me a village in Colombia needs our help building a medical clinic, a school, some homes, and a couple of barns. They'd been burned out when locals refused to grow marijuana and poppy plants for drug lords."*

*Gideon lifted his hands as if to indicate the next part was a surprise to him. "And the Boss says that he's sending me down there to spearhead the operation. And I'm like, who is he talkin' to? Me? No way! I'm just one of the small-time trim operators on second shift. But he says, yeah, it's gonna be me, and I try to talk him out of it, but it only gets worse. He tells* *me to select three hundred of our people to go with me. And I say that if we're gonna hold off drug lords <u>and</u> build a village, we're gonna need at least two thousand guys. But the Boss says not to worry about it because he's got a plan...."*

Judas rolled his eyes and moved away. He remembered that whole undertaking and what it had taken from their bottom line last year. This company needed a CEO who was a pragmatist, a realist, a person who wasn't always turning the other cheek, walking the extra mile, and giving away his extra coat.

Judas rounded a small clump of trees and found his way blocked. In front of him folks seated on blankets were eating hamburgers and munching french fries while listening to Noah Clayton's story.

*"Okay, I love the Boss—who among us doesn't?" said Noah. "But, let's face it, he can come up with some really wild schemes at times, folks. And the reason you haven't seen me for more than a year is because of one of these schemes. I know you probably saw on the national news some of what I'm about to tell you, but wait till I fill you in on the whole scoop. It goes back to an afternoon when I got summoned to the front office."*

Noah paused in thought as if recalling that day. *"The Boss says that in about a year there's going to be a severe tropical cyclone that will hit an island off the coast of India. How he knows stuff like that, don't ask me. I've just learned to go with it. At any rate, there's going to be this huge tropical cyclone,* *he tells me, and he wants to make sure that the plants and animals that are indigenous to that island—*indigenous *being something I had to look up—aren't lost for eternity. So, he tells me he's rented the largest airplane hangar on the island, and he's sending me and my crew over there to build a boat."*

*Noah scratched his head. "I said, 'We're building a boat inside of an airplane hangar?' and he says yeah, because this is going to be the biggest boat that island has ever seen. It's going to have cages and stables and corrals and paddocks and even its own pond inside. And I asked him, 'What are we going to put inside that boat?' and he says, 'A set of everything.' And as it turns out, he wasn't kidding." Noah paused, then added, "Course, he never does kid about stuff like that, does he? So, I asked, 'Well, how exactly are we...?'"*

*Judas cringed when he thought of the Sri Lanka "ordeal." They had saved the precious little monkeys and birds and even the snakes, but at an outrageous cost. He had shown Jesus the numbers, had explained the loss of manpower to the plant, had pleaded for some common-sense analysis of such a project, but, no, the plan had gone ahead as projected. Oh, if only he, Judas, the one straight-thinking person on the whole management team, could be given the reins of this company, within six months it would be an entirely new operation.*

*At last he spotted Jesus. Judas stepped through the enclave of picnic guests as if they were nothing more than squatters and hastened toward the large fire pit where Jesus was supervising the frying of fish. Without turning around, Jesus asked, "Hungry, Judas? I've got the coals just right. What's your pleasure—perch or blue gill?"*

*"Aw, baloney," said Judas in disgust.*

*"Abalone coming right up," said Jesus. "Got some just about ready here."*

*Judas was not amused. "I'm not here for fried fish or cake walks or bean-bag throws. Your charitable ventures this past year have set us back in our growth plans. We need to take steps to get us pointed in the right direction again."*

*"*<u>*Whose*</u>* growth plans, friend?" Jesus asked, turning slowly. "To what end? Look around you. These people are happy. They know they're part of something bigger than themselves. They have stories to share, projects to tell about, dreams to explore. They couldn't care less about balance sheets."*

*"Someone has to care," insisted Judas. "And most of the time, it winds up being me…and me alone."*

*Jesus looked intently at Judas. "You have one of the sharpest minds in our entire company. The problem is, you have one of the dullest hearts. Don't let your heart be troubled. Believe in me. I know what I'm doing."*

*Judas struggled to lift his oversized briefcase and open it while still standing. He extracted sheaths of papers. "But this latest venture of yours. If it goes wrong, it could kick the pins out from underneath the whole company."*

*"It won't go wrong," responded Jesus, as he motioned for his helpers to turn the fish on the grill.*

*"Oh, but <u>really</u>," insisted Judas, "sending Nehemiah Mason to rebuild floodwalls and dikes in the Ukraine? It's ridiculous. We started out strictly in the carpentry business, and now you've gotten us into concrete, earthmoving, steel, modular fabrications—we're all over the map."*

*"Exactly," confirmed Jesus, "including the Ukraine. We'll go where we can do the most good."*

*"But the local officials don't even want us there. They've threatened to destroy the entire project."*

*"They're too greedy for that," said Jesus. "When they discover what the repaired levees and seawalls and harbors will do for their economy, they'll allow our supervisors and their citizens to finish the projects. Remember how it worked out when we were rebuilding that village in Colombia? You were against that project, too, but it turned out fine."*

*Judas rolled his eyes, resignedly returned the papers, and closed the briefcase. "You said that you'd eventually turn the operation of the whole company over to the twelve of us on the management team. Will my hands be tied then, too?"*

*"Your <u>hands</u>?" said Jesus. He looked at Judas with a genuinely sad expression. "No, not your <u>hands</u>."*

*Jesus turned, called some last-minute instructions to the men grilling the fish, and then signaled to Paul Stoner on the other side of the lawn. "It's time," he called. "Gather everyone, please."*

*Paul signaled to Pete, Jonathan, Beau, Barney, Matt, Danni, Martha, and Andy, who were stationed at various points around the company property, to encourage the employees and their families to congregate at a central area where Jesus stood waiting for them. For the next ten minutes, the people picked up their belongings and moved closer to the central area in front of Jesus. Many brought the remainder of their picnic food with them and resumed eating as they relaxed on the lawn and waited for Jesus to give his traditional yearly talk before the day ended and everyone went home.*

*"Let me begin by saying this will be my last talk to all of you as a group," Jesus announced. Murmurs swept through the crowd, but he quelled them with his raised hands. "From the beginning I made it clear that I would spend three years training a management team to take over the work after I stepped aside. Soon, that time of transition will be upon us."*

*He began to walk slowly among the people. "Before departing, however, I want to take time to remind each of you what this company is all about...what we are all about. I've watched you these past few years. You've become a family. When one of you suffered a loss and was in mourning, others provided comfort. Do continue. That's as it should be." He pointed out certain employees in the crowd. "I've seen many, <u>many</u> of you improve greatly in your skills, even when I had to push you out of your comfort zones."*

*Several people nodded and laughed about that, recognizing themselves as examples.*

*"Nevertheless," Jesus continued, "you've remained humble about your accomplishments and have even been gracious in giving advice and guidance to others not yet as far along as you are. Because of that attitude, I'm going to designate company stock to many of you so you can inherit this company."*

The employees looked at one another, smiling in amazement at this news. Calls of, "Thanks, Boss," and "Wow, that's great" rose from the crowd.

Jesus continued. *"Because of your work, you have brought peace to many places in the world. You've rebuilt destroyed villages and towns and reconstructed their schools, homes, and businesses. In many places you've shown the local residents how to melt weapons and turn them into farming tools. I want you to continue to be peacemakers. You'll be blessed in your efforts."*

"It hasn't always been easy, Boss," someone at the back of the crowd called out.

Jesus smiled. *"I'm very aware of that. Conglomerates have tried to take us over. Foreign governments have tried to expel us. Competitors have tried to sabotage our operations. The media have spent equal time glorifying and vilifying us. Some of us have lost friends or had family members turn against us. Many of you have suffered indignity because of my name and because of what we stand for. But you've remained the salt of the earth and the light of the world. I'm proud of you, and I want you—this company—to remain a beacon to others. Even when I move on, my presence will still be here among you. Never forget that."*

*Jesus waved, signaling that his talk was over. His closest associates, as usual, moved in and tried to form a bit of a protective barrier around him as he left the crowd. When they had gained some distance, they paused, and each man, in turn, shook the hand of Jesus and thanked him for the fun they had had that day, for another year of friendship and encouragement, and for his trust in them.*

*Judas was the last to approach Jesus. "I know I'm often the odd man out in our plans and debates and discussions. But I do love you as a brother. We see things differently, and I'm sure I'll continue to be a thorn in your side, but I'm glad I've had this chance to be with you."*

*Jesus looked at Judas for a moment before pulling him forward, kissing him on the forehead, and releasing him. Then Jesus turned and walked away.*

## There Is No Such Thing as Insignificant Improvement

We'll call her "Belinda." She came into my university office and slumped into a chair.

"It didn't work," she announced. "I read your book, Doc. I set my goal, broke it into measurable units, created a system of attack, and went at it with my whole heart. And …I failed."

I raised my eyebrows questioningly. "Backtrack a moment," I said. "Tell me about this goal."

Belinda shifted slightly in her seat. "The thirty-fifth-year reunion of my high school graduating class is set for two weeks from now," she began. "I got the announcement last September, just after I'd finished reading your book.

***The Power of Positive Productivity.*** I set a goal to lose forty pounds before that reunion."

"And?"

"*And* I joined a fitness center, hired a trainer, and worked my hinder off—literally—for ten months," she asserted. "I was determined that in spite of having had three kids and being thirty-five years older, I was going to my reunion at the same weight I'd been on graduation day. But, I failed. In spite of my total commitment, I've lost only twenty-four pounds. I'm utterly depressed."

I scribbled some numbers on a pad, then looked up.

"Let me say this back to you. Since last September you've been losing two or three pounds every month, you've been developing muscle tone, you've vastly improved your cardiovascular system, and you've increased your physical strength and level of energy…yet, you think you're a *failure* because you still need half a year to hit your target weight?"

Belinda titled her head slightly, suddenly considering a new perspective on her previously conceived "failure."

I pressed the issue. "You've taken three bowling balls of weight off your body, and you call that failure? Your legs are firm, your neck has no flab, and your arms are strong. That's failure? Hey, I suggest you go look at photos of yourself at this time *last* summer. Would you want to swap bodies with *that* woman?" I paused. "Well, would you?"

Belinda had to smile. "No," she admitted. "I guess I like the new me much better." After a moment her smile grew bigger. "And so does my husband."

I nodded my understanding. "Look," I said, "a positive attitude is vital to success, but it has to be balanced with common sense. Goals cannot be so outrageous that they only depress you with their impossibility. The goal you set last September was attainable and worthwhile. Losing pounds steadily each month is a sane, healthy way to become reconditioned. You *will* reach your goal. You just need to log a few more months of work."

Belinda pondered that a moment, then grimaced. "I see your point, Doc," she said, "but I've got to confess. I really, *really* wanted to go back to that reunion looking the way I did when I graduated. That's probably vanity, but I can't help feeling that way."

I shrugged. "Sure, we all wish we could turn back the hands of time. But you need to judge yourself fairly. Be honest. Is there anyone in your graduating class who has not aged another thirty-five years?"

"Well, no, I guess everyone has aged the same as me."

"And have any of the *other* prom queens or pom-pom girls or cheerleaders had babies? Are there any other gals from your class who might have a few stretch marks or maybe a bit of middle-age spread?"

"Hmmm...no doubt," Belinda conceded. "I'm probably not alone in that boat."

"Of course you aren't. What you've accomplished in the past ten months is amazing. Reunion or no reunion, you've improved your health, established new disciplines, and revitalized your whole being."

Belinda sat up straighter. "I have, haven't I? Wow, I've been beating myself up for no reason. I've already succeeded, and I'll just continue to succeed even more."

"Precisely," I affirmed. "Always keep one thing in mind: *There is no such thing as insignificant improvement.* Improvement is just that—*improvement!*

## Proper Perspective

Within all of us glimmers the spark of desire to improve ourselves. For Belinda, the motivation was her desire to look good at her class reunion. Other folks have different but equally valid motivations. Drake worked a second job for seven years and paid off his home thirteen years early because he desired a sense of security. Cynthia spent four years listening to language tapes so that she would qualify for a management position with one of her company's South American divisions. Aaron followed a three-year program of power walking, jogging, and then running so he could participate in marathons with his two growing sons.

Unfortunately, too many people look at what seems to be the ultimate goal, find it too daunting, and thereafter refuse to make an effort to achieve any part of it. They need a new perspective.

You've heard the bromides: "Inch by inch, anything's a cinch," and "Well begun is half done," and "The longest journey begins with just one step." As corny as they may sound, they contain truth. The trick to achieving any goal is to get started. You have to kick in gear, realizing that no matter how small your effort might be, it truly is better than nothing.

Let me explain with a real-life example. Mike came to me, explained that he was $3,000 in debt to a credit card company that was charging him 18 percent interest. Each month he was paying $45 of interest and making no progress toward getting free of this financial burden. He said he'd been hoping to get overtime at work so he could slap a huge amount of cash against his debt, but his company had been able to give him only about three hours of overtime per week.

"Do you have any discretionary money in your budget each payday?" I asked.

Mike looked puzzled by the question but said yes, he usually spent about ten dollars on lotto tickets each Saturday. It was just a hobby, a bit of gambling and gamesmanship.

"Stop doing that," I said. "Instead, put one dollar a day all month directly against your debt."

"One dollar a day?" asked Mike. "*One* dollar? What good will that do me?"

I got out some paper and a pocket calculator and showed him. "At a buck a day, you'll knock off $30 from your debt the first month. Your balance will be down to $2,970. That means your interest payment will go down by about fifty cents. The next month you'll be down to $2,940, and you can throw on that fifty cents of saved interest, too."

"Doesn't seem like much progress," Mike argued.

"At first, maybe not," I agreed, "but look at the long-range results. If you pay *nothing* per day against principal, after ten years you'll still be $3,000 in debt and you'll have given the credit card company $4,500 in interest payments. But if you pay down the debt by a dollar a day, you'll be debt free in five years, *and* you will have saved another $3,000 in interest you didn't have to pay out."

Mike was stunned. "At a dollar a day? That measly amount of money?"

"Yes," I said, showing him the paperwork. "The tiniest bit of progress winds up being a *major* improvement, if you'll just get started and stay at it."

Mike went over the numbers several times, then looked up at me. "From now on, lotto is out, and this sure bet is in!"

## Gauging Progress

In making incremental progress, one key factor you must keep in mind is that the only benchmark of improvement that counts is a comparison of where you are now as opposed to where you used to be. Never worry about how rich or skinny or muscular or well-dressed or highly educated or famous someone else is.

Other people are not your point of reference. You are evaluating progress only by examining your own circumstances. If today you are $30 less in debt than you were a month ago, *that's* what counts. Forget about your brother-in-law who brags about paying cash for his new car. That has nothing to do with you. *You* are focused on *you*, and any improvement you make in *your* life is what you need to measure progress by.

But how, you may wonder, do you find the motivation that will inspire you to take the first baby step toward improvement? Let me make three suggestions.

***Consider scaring yourself.*** Fear is a great motivator. It can be used as a positive force. When used rationally and believably, fear can radically alter your life. You might say to yourself, "If I don't quit smoking, I'll never live to see my grandchildren graduate from high school and college." Or, you might say, "If I don't start getting up earlier in the mornings and stop racing to get to work, I'm going to wind up in a serious accident one day." Whatever it takes to deliver a wake-up call to yourself, find it, repeat it often, and take steps to eliminate it.

***Make a benefits list.*** Sit and write a worthy and challenging goal at the top of a piece of paper or a new electronic document. List *all* the potential benefits you might gain by accomplishing even *part* of that goal.

You might write, "Wean Myself from My TV and Video Game Addictions." Beneath that you might make a list that includes, "More quality time with my spouse, kids and friends…less eating of junk food…catching up on letter writing…more time for exercise…less stress over depressing world news…reduced eye strain…chance to develop a hobby…do more home repairs and yard work… wax the car…catch a nap…do community service…read a classic book." The overwhelming positive impact that striving for this goal will have on you will motivate you to make *some* effort toward its achievement. At first, you may cut out just one silly half-hour sitcom or video game per evening, but that will still give you three and a half hours a week of additional free time for other projects. Amazing! A little suddenly becomes a lot!

***Dedicate your progress to someone else.*** Think of someone you truly love, admire, or desire to please, and then throw yourself into accomplishing your goal as either a benefit to that person or as a tribute to him or her. Investing ourselves in people helps others, but it also is a personal blessing. This can be used as an improvement motivator.

For example, Suzanne had always wanted to earn a graduate degree but had put it off due to expense, time, and other commitments. However, after she gave birth to her first child, she started taking one grad school class per semester. Suzanne's friends said, "At that rate, it'll take you five years to do the course work and write your master's thesis. That's too long to drag out." But Suzanne would not be deterred. She saw one class per semester as *significant* improvement. Five years later, she graduated with an MA degree, double-majoring in child psychology and elementary education, just in time to begin homeschooling her five-year-old child. That had been her goal all along. By wanting to improve the life of her child, she had simultaneously improved her own life.

## Steady Progress

A story is told of a sixteen-year-old farm boy whose father gave him a newborn calf. The boy lifted the calf over a fence every morning so it could graze. Two years later the boy could lift a full-grown cow over the fence. Indeed, maybe he only improved his weight lifting by a few more ounces a day—but that's all it took. There is no such thing as insignificant improvement or progress.

Whatever your dream goal is, you should regularly take *some* step toward it. What you now understand is, even if you never attain the entire goal, *whatever* you achieve toward it will vastly improve your life. The effort itself is rewarding.

Start improving. Take a step. ***Now!***

## Key Points Found in Section 5

1. There is no such thing as insignificant improvement.

2. Within all of us, just waiting for the right wind of motivation to fan it into full blaze, glimmers the spark of desire to improve ourselves.

3. The trick to achieving any goal is to get started.

4. No matter how small your effort may be, it's better than nothing.

5. The only benchmark that counts is where you are now as opposed to where you used to be.

6. Consider scaring yourself . . . making a benefits list. . . dedicating your improvement to someone else.

*From a second-floor observation platform, John Brothers looked down upon a large group of young workers on the plant's main floor, all busy doing assembly work. "One's missing," he said.*

*Judas looked up from the calculator on his mobile phone. "Say what?"*

*"There are supposed to be a hundred trainees working down there, but I count only ninety-nine."*

*Judas shrugged. "We can still hit quota. No problem."*

*John turned. "It's not the quota I'm concerned about. It's the missing worker. You know what the boss's priority would be if he were here."*

*Judas narrowed his eyes. "Well, he's* not *here. And I am. And this part of the operation is my domain, so I'm not going to lose valuable time searching for some misfit who should never have been hired in the first place." He turned his attention back to his calculator and resumed punching in numbers.*

*"Hiring isn't your responsibility," said John. "It's not your company. The boss can hire whomever he chooses to hire."*

*Judas moved to the railing. "Look at them. Ten are blind, seven are in wheelchairs, three are deaf, and every one of them was in abject poverty until they started working here.*

105

How am I supposed to run an assembly line when all he'll let me hire are 'the lame and the needy'?"

"Seems to be working," said John. "You just told me you'd make quota today—even shorthanded."

"Don't mock me. If I had the right people, I could double our output. I've run the numbers, done the time studies. I know what I'm talking about. Give me the money to buy computer-programmed lathes and let me bring in workers who aren't crippled, and I'll show you a profit margin that'll make your eyes pop out."

"You know what the boss says about gaining the whole world."

"We're not gaining even a piece of it. Look—between you and me—I've had some private meetings with a group of foreign investors. They like my ideas. They agree that...."

"Wait a second! Say that again. You've gone behind the boss's back and conspired to sell the company? Are you kidding?"

"Hold on, hold on. It's not like that. I'm just trying to think about what would be best for all of us."

"All of us? Meaning who? Me? Matt? Pete? Andy? Barney? I don't remember anybody complaining about the company's profit margin. You're thinking about you. You've had dollar signs dancing in front of your eyes ever since you joined us."

*"And thank goodness I have. Somebody needs to get his head out of the clouds and apply some business standards to this place. Half the time—including today—*he's *off somewhere incommunicado. That's no way for a CEO to run a company."*

*"You know he's more than just a businessman. Besides, he told us right from the beginning, back when we started with him three years ago, that one day he'd be turning over the whole operation to us. When he goes off for a few days to do others things, it helps prepare us for the time when he won't be returning."*

*"I can hardly—"* Judas caught himself. *"Soon enough,"* he mumbled.

*"So, who is it?"* John pointed. *"Who's missing down there?"*

*"What am I, the truant officer?"*

John smiled sardonically. *"You're the Gestapo. You scroll those electronic time cards every morning. You know who's here, when each one clocked in, and who's missing. Did you know that behind your back they call you Judas I-scare-a-lot?"*

*"Droll."* Judas thumbed his smartphone. *"Bethany Darda. She should have clocked in at eight, but she never showed up. I've notified Accounting to dock her a day's pay."*

*"I'm sure you have."* John pulled out his own phone. *"Send her home address to me. We need to make sure she's okay."*

"We! Oh, no, not me. I've got inventory to tally, billing statements to send out, and—in case you hadn't noticed—a crew of ninety-nine to tend. One straggler just isn't that important to the total operation around here."

John closed the distance between them. "What is it with you? Haven't you learned anything these past three years? You should listen to yourself. You talk crazy." He let out a breath. "We don't use computerized lathes because we do high-quality handmade work. We hire people with physical challenges because they are no less valuable than any of the rest of us. And we worry when one of us goes missing because people are more important than profits."

Judas stepped back. "Wow! The thunder booms!" He sniffed indignantly. "You don't need to lecture me on company values. At least my mommy didn't show up asking the boss to make me his right-hand man."

John ignored the comment and moved toward the stairwell. "Follow me."

Judas shook his head. "Gees, now you're even sounding like him. What next? You plan to grow a beard?" He hurried to catch up.

When they reached the main floor, John began asking the workers if anyone knew Bethany Darda. Everyone was acquainted with her, but no one knew why she hadn't reported for work. One girl finally said, "She wasn't ready when the van came to pick her up today. Bethany's blind, like me. We ride a shuttle."

*John whirled on Judas. "She's* <u>blind</u>*? Bethany can't see? Why didn't you tell me that?"*

*Judas shrugged. "I don't play favorites. Come to work, you get paid. Don't come to work, you don't get paid. Blind or not, it makes no difference to me."*

*"Well, it makes a difference to me. Come on. We'll use my car."*

*Judas waved a hand. "And what about these dear folks? Who's going to supervise them if I leave?"*

*John lifted his voice. "Can you people keep things going if we leave long enough to check on Bethany?"*

*To a person, positive responses were heard from every direction.*

*"They'll be fine," said John. "Lock your phone's GPS on Bethany's address. Let's go."*

*The drive took thirty minutes, and Judas was sullen most of the way. Finally, looking bored, he asked, "What'd you do before this?"*

*"Me? I thought you knew. James and I worked for our dad, a commercial fisherman. We went for it all. You know, sunfish, salmon, cod. But a few summers ago we had a bad spell. Tropical storms messed up the migration of the fish. We couldn't catch a thing. We were going bust."*

*"Turn left at the next corner."*

*"So, one day we're coming in from another long day with no luck. We look up, and some guy is just standing in the*

*middle of the ocean on this tiny, tiny atoll. We veered over and helped him aboard. It was the boss."*

*"How'd he get way out there?"*

*John laughed. "We asked him that. He said he walked."*

*Judas frowned. "I hate when he does that. He says he never lies and then he constantly makes those silly remarks. Walked!"*

*"Anyway, he told us he was starting a new business and he was hiring. He wanted to know if we needed work. Needed work! My dad's boat was about to be repossessed, James and I were flat broke, and we hadn't had a decent meal in a week. So, we said yeah, we needed jobs, but we didn't know squat about building furniture. And that's when he said it was more a business about building people than building furniture, and he'd show us how to become people builders."*

*"Really? And what'd your old man say to that?"*

*"Not much he could say. He hadn't been able to pay us anything, and, hey, work is work, right?" He paused a moment in recollection. "And...well, the boss added a deal sweetener."*

*"Pull in by that curb. What do you mean by a deal sweetener?"*

*"Okay, I know this is going to sound crazy, but the boss told my dad that if he'd let James and me leave with him the next day, he'd help dad bring in the catch of a lifetime. He told my dad to turn the boat around and go back out to sea a couple of miles and then to cast the nets off the starboard side."*

*"I thought you said you'd already come up empty out there."*

*"Only too true. But my dad was a bit freaked out by a guy who could just 'appear' in the middle of the ocean. He was kind of afraid not to do it. So, we turned around and went back out and lowered the nets."*

*"And...?"*

*"And we started pulling in so many fish, we nearly swamped the boat. We were out there for three hours until we were overflowing with fish, and the nets were breaking by then anyway from the overloads. We slogged back to port, and dad cashed in."*

*"This is true? Not some kind of fish story?"* Judas opened the door and got out.

*"Of course it's true. You've been with the boss three years. You've seen him in action. If not, I'd never have told you about it. I mean who else could believe...?"*

*"Yeah, yeah. He's a grandstander all right. But one of these days he's going to take it too far. I plan to be on the right side of the fence when that happens."*

John stared. *"You know, you really worry me when you talk like that. If you hate what we're doing at the company so much, why did you join us in the first place?"*

*"I sometimes wonder that myself. Here, this is the girl's address. What now?"*

*"I stand at the door and knock."*

"Stop doing that!" Judas rapped lightly against the frame of the unpainted door. He waited ten seconds. "Okay, nobody's home. Let's go."

John doubled his fist and pounded four times against the wobbly door. A faint cry could be heard inside the house. The two men looked at each other. Simultaneously, they both reached for the door handle.

John entered first. "Bethany? Bethany! It's John Brothers. Where are you?"

"Back here. I need help."

John raced toward the back of the house. He passed threadbare furnishings, torn window shades, and banged-up appliances. Judas followed, but at a more cautious pace, as though expecting to be mugged by a hidden assailant.

John found Bethany huddled next to the body of a girl of about twelve. "What…what happened here?"

"It's Tabby, my little sister," said Bethany. "I can't make her wake up. I've tried everything. I've shaken her, called her name…she always gets up and gets me ready for work."

As soon as Judas entered the room, he walked over and felt for a pulse. Then looked at John and shook his head.

Gently, John touched Bethany's arm and said, "Let's get out of here, Bethany. We'll call someone about your sister."

"We don't have a phone. Our mom comes and goes. She hasn't been around for more than a week."

"We have phones. Come on."

"*But what about Tabby?*"

*There was a pause, then Judas said, "I'm sorry, Bethany, but your sister is dead."*

*"What? No! No, she's not! She has epilepsy and sometimes has fits. But she's not dead."*

*"Yes," Judas responded flatly. "Your sister is dead. No movement. No pulse. She's definitely dead."*

*A voice behind them said, "No. She's not."*

*Judas and John turned quickly. Jesus stood in the doorway.*

*"Boss!" said John. "How did you...?"*

*"I walked," said Jesus. He moved across the room and looked down at the motionless girl.*

*"She's gone," said Judas. "I checked her neck and wrist. No heartbeat. Her lips are blue. She's dead."*

*Jesus shifted slightly and looked into Judas's eyes. "She's not the one who's dead. Leave the room, please."*

*Judas blinked, then slowly made to exit. John moved to follow, but Jesus raised a hand and said, "You stay, John."*

*John returned to Bethany's side and put his arm around her shoulders. "A friend is here. He's going to examine your sister."*

*"Who?"*

*"The man we work for."*

*Jesus bent over. He stretched out his hand and said, "Get up now, Tabitha."*

*The young girl's eyelids fluttered. She squinted a moment until her eyes focused on Jesus. She looked from his face to Bethany's and back again. When Jesus stretched out his hand to help her up, she hesitated. But as he continued to smile, she let him pull her to her feet. Once steady, she turned to Bethany and nodded in the direction of Jesus and John.*

*"Friends of yours?" she asked.*

*Elated, Bethany replied, "Yeah, yeah. From work. Are you okay, Tabby?"*

*"I'm hungry."*

*Jesus smiled. "John?"*

*"Yes, sir?"*

*"Drop this young lady off at her school and go in and explain to her principal that she had a medical issue, but she's going to be perfectly fine from now on. Then take Bethany back to join the ninety and nine. On the way, pull in somewhere and get them breakfast."*

*"Will do, Boss."*

*"Good." Then, as an afterthought, Jesus said, "Oh, and tell Judas to cancel that order for three computerized lathes." He smiled. "Not much gets by Matt Feingold."*

*John nodded. "And nothing gets by you." Something suddenly occurred to him. "How are you going to get to work, Boss? Can we give you lift back across the bridge?"*

*"No thanks," said Jesus. "I'll walk."*

## Section 6

# The Secret of Rapid Advancement:
## Attitude

More than fifty years ago a popular song called "High Hopes" chronicled an ant that moved a rubber tree plant and a ram that punched a hole in a concrete dam. Although told repeatedly that what they were attempting was impossible, the ant and ram persisted and prevailed.

I won't go so far as to say that I believe an ant can move a rubber tree plant, but I will say that a positive attitude often inspires achievements that seem virtually impossible. In my opinion, the greatest motivational book ever written was *The Little Engine That Could*. (I gave each of my grandchildren a copy at birth.) I say this because, in my work as a reporter, interviewer, and motivation researcher, I have repeatedly discovered among high-end achievers a marvelous naïveté that they summarized as, "I did it because I didn't know it couldn't be done."

Loretta Lynn told me, "My husband and I got in our old car with boxes of my first recording. We started driving from town to town, just barging in on disc jockeys and program directors. We asked if I could be interviewed on the air and if they'd play my record. Most said okay. Months later our record company executives said, 'You can't do that. You need press agents, publicists, and managers to prepare a national strategy for promoting your record.' But by then it was too late. My record was already in the national top ten. Praise the Lord for blind ambition."

Similarly, Daryle Doden, founder of Ambassador Steel, told me, "I happened upon a guy who needed to buy some steel and a guy who wanted to sell some steel. I worked out the details and closed the deal. I had a knack for it, so I did it again. And again. A year later a professional metals broker told me, 'You need to understand the fine points of contracts, the engineering construction of steel girders, and the transfer routes of trucks and trains in order to succeed in this business.' But by then I was already a millionaire with a large base of customers."

## Why Confidence Counts

I discovered something amazing about attitude when I entered the Army. On the first day of basic training our drill sergeant burst into our barracks and bellowed, "At-ten-tion!" We all snapped to. The sergeant, arrayed in his circular Mountie hat, starched fatigues, and spit-shined boots, strode between the two rows of green recruits. Steadily, boisterously, affirmatively, he began to dictate to us how we would dress, when we would eat, where we would train, and how we would talk. None of us argued or contradicted or even questioned anything this man said. From his demeanor, volume, and posture, it was completely understood that he was in charge.

Now, why was this so amazing? Well, consider the situation for what it really was. There were sixty men in that room and, at the time (1971) the draft was still in effect. I later learned that twenty-seven of those men had college degrees and nine even had a master's degree; five of these men came from multimillionaire families; three of the men were perfectly bilingual; fifteen had been star athletes in high school or college; one was the son of a congressman; another guy's dad was a police chief in a major Midwestern city; one guy was a licensed pilot; three were certified scuba divers; and two fellows had CPA certifications.

The drill sergeant had seen all of our personnel files before he'd ever laid eyes on us. He knew all of these facts about our high levels of education, wealth, and the diversity of talent in that room. Conversely, the sergeant had never gotten past high school; he was earning only a modest income; and he certainly had no connection with prestigious people or families. For all intents and purposes, he should have been overwhelmingly intimidated by this group of sixty young men.

But he wasn't.

He wasn't intimidated because he knew one all-empowering secret: *You can't beat a man at his own game.*

The sergeant was on *his* turf, playing by *his* rules. He was dominating us by tapping into his superior knowledge and experience in the only arena that now counted. Oh, sure, some of us fellows could quote Shakespeare and work algebra and define the branches of the federal government. But what good would any of that do us in five months when we would find ourselves in the jungles of Vietnam—where forty-five of us actually wound up?

The drill sergeant was a master of engaging in hand-to-hand combat; cleaning, loading and firing the M16 rifle; applying emergency first-aid procedures; jumping out of helicopters; wearing camouflage; and living off the land. He was confident because he knew he was top dog in this setting.

There's a real lesson in this: By becoming an absolute master of some area of expertise, you never have to feel second-rate to anyone.

### Improving Attitude

Human nature being what it is, many people have poor attitudes about their personal potential. There can be many reasons for this—negative parents or siblings, discouraging teachers, early setbacks or failures, physical disabilities, poverty, and perhaps even cultural limitations.

Ironically, people born to advantage *also* can grow up with negative attitudes about themselves. I've met people with so much money, they can never tell if anyone likes them for themselves or just for their money. This inhibits them socially and economically. I've also met people with genius IQs who have gone through life as social outcasts, nerds, dweebs, weirdoes, and intellectual loners because they've lacked the confidence to be comfortable with and confident about their talents.

It becomes quickly obvious that a positive attitude is not an automatic endowment. Quite the opposite. A positive attitude must be developed, nurtured, reinforced, and sustained. It requires mental conditioning. In striving for this, we can learn some lessons and gain some new perspectives from successful people with positive attitudes.

**Someone has to be first, so why not me?** There were no African-American Major League baseball players until Jackie Robinson. There were no female astronauts until Sally Ride. There were no college drop-out billionaires until Bill Gates. There were no disabled presidents until Franklin D. Roosevelt. There were no blind honors graduates of Radcliff College until Helen Keller. *Someone* always has to be "first" in every breakthrough endeavor.

The primary requirement of a positive mental attitude is a belief that cultural or social hardships (gender, race, ethnicity, age, education) cannot be used as excuses for self-limitation. That's all mere window dressing. If, for example, height or bulk were criteria for success in Hollywood, Mickey Rooney and Woody Allen and Danny DeVito would never have starred in dozens of major movies. It's important to understand that success can be attained by anyone who has a strong work ethic, a purposeful life goal, and a positive mental attitude.

***If it can be done on a small scale, why not on a large scale?*** Next-level thinking can take a kid from sandlot ball to Little League to Pony League to the Minor Leagues to the Major Leagues. High-level success very often is attained via incremental advances. One's attitude about one's total potential for success in any area of endeavor is greatly enhanced by sustained benchmarks of success, even if they seem minor at first.

"Sure, I had an early desire to become a best-selling author," says Jerry B. Jenkins, whose *Left Behind* series has sold more than sixty million books. "But I had to reinforce that dream by getting my name into print any way I could do so when I first started. I wrote sports stories for the hometown paper, then articles for small magazines, then short works of fiction for teens, and finally the series that put me on the *New York Times* best-seller list a dozen times. Each time my byline appeared in print, it sent a message of success to my brain. It kept me moving forward, believing in my ability to become a best-selling author."

***To be a picture of success, I need a success picture.*** A person's self-perception can be changed from negative to positive by focusing constantly on an image of excellence. Paul J. Meyer frequently told the story of a prince who was born humpbacked. He commissioned a sculptor to make a statue of him, only showing himself as being erect and strong. The finished statue was placed outside the prince's window where he would see it every day. Whenever he looked at it, he tried to emulate it. In time, he was no longer stooped-shouldered.

That story is not as farfetched as one might believe. In his research into the psychodynamics of self-improvement, Dr. Maxwell Maltz documented an amazing phenomenon. People would come to him for cosmetic surgery, and Dr. Maltz would make a prominent nose smaller or drooping eyelids tighter or a misaligned jaw straighter. Amazingly, as he met these people for follow-up appointments at three, six, nine, and twelve-month intervals, he discovered that many had gotten job promotions, had started meeting new friends and dating, had lost weight and were enjoying vastly improved overall health, had started dressing in nicer clothes, and had even become financially prosperous.

Once these people started seeing themselves as having become prettier and handsomer, they took on the persona of someone who was confident, relaxed, self-assured, and very much at ease with the world. This, in turn, attracted admirers and followers. The external changes of cosmetic surgery had triggered mental and emotional changes, too.

From these case studies, Dr. Maltz theorized that if a person could skip the cosmetic surgery and go directly to the altering of one's self-perception, the end results would be the same—with less pain and less expense. This proved to be true, as experiments with self-hypnosis, mental imaging, possibility thinking, and mind-mapping subsequently bore out.

Some people develop this new attitude about themselves by playing recorded messages with words of reinforcement ("I'm staying faithful to my new exercise regimen." "I know that people respect my ideas.") Some people have used computerized photo modification software to create photos of themselves as they would look if thirty-five pounds lighter. They put copies on their refrigerator, bathroom mirrors, and even vehicle dashboards. Whatever it takes, creating a new mental image will result in a positive, upbeat self-inspiring attitude. This, in time, will give anyone an edge in life.

**You're #1**

Whether it's Mohammed Ali proclaiming, "I am the greatest" or that Little Engine saying, "I think I can, I think I can," attitude plays a key role in everyone's success or failure in life. If your attitude is less than positive, use the tenets found in this section to alter it. Your attitude will determine your altitude. It was William James who stated, "The greatest discovery of my generation is that human beings can alter their lives by altering their attitudes of mind. As you think, so shall you be."

So, think positively, and be all that you can be.

## Key Points Found in Section 6

1. Attitude provides the edge needed for success.

2. You can't beat a person at his or her own game unless you work at it just as hard.

3. By becoming an absolute master of some area of expertise, you never have to feel second-rate to anyone.

4. A positive mental attitude is not a natural endowment. It must be developed, nurtured, reinforced, and sustained.

5. Someone has to be first, so why not you?

6. The primary requirement of a positive mental attitude is a belief that cultural or social hardships cannot be used as excuses for self-limitations.

7. If it can be done on a small scale, why not on a large scale?

8. High-level success is often attained via incremental advances.

9. To be a picture of success, you need a success picture.

Charlie Archer, weary and older than his years, leaned his weight against the bus station's swinging metal door and pushed it open. He entered the small waiting room, with its rickety wooden benches, dented vending machines, and faded travel posters. Charlie's nostrils were immediately assaulted by the commingled aromas of diesel fumes, stale coffee, and human sweat. He scanned the room and was caught off-guard by the sight of the owner of the company he worked for. They locked eyes, and Jesus waved for Charlie to come over and sit by him.

"What? What're you doin' here, Boss?"

Jesus smiled. "Same as you, Charlie. Waiting for the buses to arrive."

Charlie eased himself onto the bench beside his employer. For a full moment he was speechless. "I never saw you here before," Charlie said at last. "Meetin' someone particular?"

"Many people travel long roads coming to me," said Jesus. "Even people like your Albert."

Charlie blanched and drew back immediately. His eyes widened in true amazement. "But how…?"

"So, how long has it been since he left town, Charlie? Nigh onto five years, wouldn't you say?"

*Charlie leaned forward in defeat, resting his head in his hands. Almost inaudibly he mumbled, "Four years, ten months, and nine days."*

*Jesus nodded. "And no phone calls, no e-mails, no postcards. Total silence."*

*"Not a word," confirmed Charlie in the same low voice. After a moment he looked up quizzically. "Did my wife call you or something? Oh, wow...I'm really sorry if she...."*

*"No. I was called, but not by Shirley. I just wanted to offer you some support. It's been a long, lonely vigil, coming here night after night, hoping Albert will step off the next bus, ready to return home and be part of the family again. You're a good dad."*

*Charlie shook his head. "No, no, I've failed my son. If I knew where he was, I'd go find him. If he'd contact me, I'd send him money. Truth is...I don't know if he's even still alive."*

*"He is," said Jesus, without wavering.*

*Charlie tapped his chest. "Yeah, here in my heart, no matter what, he'll always be alive. That's true enough. But I just wish I could see him again, touch him, tell him how sorry I am. It's been my continuous prayer for years. My knees are worn out."*

*"Prayers are answered in miraculous ways," said Jesus, placing a hand on Charlie's slumped shoulders. "God's hand is not so short that he cannot reach out and touch you. His ear isn't deaf so that he can't hear you."*

*"What? Even here? Now?"*

*"Definitely even now," said Jesus.*

*Charlie pondered that momentarily, then said, "Kids. Hard to understand, y'know? Tried my best to give 'em everything they could ever want. Herman, Albert's twin, was always the serious one. Good grades, class president, varsity debate team. Never a lick of trouble...but he's always had an edge. Like he's suspicious of everyone. Mind you, I love him, but we've never shared a laugh or gone camping or had confidential talks about his girlfriends or his school or his hobbies...if he even has any."*

*"Girlfriends or hobbies?"*

*"Either...neither," said Charlie. "How would I know? He's distant."*

*"Uh-huh," said Jesus. "Just like Albert."*

*Charlie straightened. He stared at Jesus, square on, first with a puzzled expression, then ever so slowly with an evolving look of dawning comprehension.*

*"Hey," he said at last, "you got somethin' there. I never thought of that before, but you're right as rain. One of my boys is just as distant from me as the other. I haven't lost one son, I've lost 'em both. I'm a miserable failure as a father, an absolute miserable failure as a father." He eased back against the wall behind the bench, looking defeated.*

*"Maybe not," said Jesus softly. "Maybe they're miserable failures as sons. They have free will, you know."*

*"I can't shake the feelin' that I'm the one to blame. It came to a head the month they graduated from high school. They may have been twins, but they couldn't have been more different. Herman would be on the honor roll, and Albert would be expelled for fightin' in the lunchroom. Herman would be offered a scholarship, and Albert would be arrested for drinking under age. I kept warning Albert that he couldn't expect me to bail him out of trouble every time. Sooner or later he'd go too far."*

*"Which he did, right?"*

*Charlie ran his fingers through his hair. He bit his lower lip, stifling tears as emotional recollections filled his mind.* "It was graduation night. Herman had given the student speech, him being the top guy and all."

*"Valedictorian."*

*"Yeah...yeah, that thing. Anyway, Albert got a diploma, too, but only by the skin of his teeth. In fact, we didn't know until the last few days if he was actually going to get to walk through the ceremonies or not. But they let him. And, instead of being grateful, he pranced around like some proud peacock, gloating like he'd pulled one over on the school or somethin'. It embarrassed me, and I thought Herman would pop a cork. Then, to make matters worse, Albert and one of his cronies boosted a car that night and went out joyriding, celebrating their freedom from high school."*

*"Wasn't too joyful, though, was it?"*

*"Naw, sure wasn't," said Charlie. "Cops picked him and the other guy up after they side-swiped a parked car. Got a call at two in the morning saying they had Albert in a holdin' cell at the county lock-up. My wife was a bundle of nerves. We'd been waitin' up for Albert to come home or to call."*

*Charlie paused, let out a long breath, then rubbed his forefinger and thumb across his forehead, as he tried to organize his memories of that night. It was a wrestling match, for he'd tried for many years to drive those memories away, yet he found himself reliving that night over and again, visualizing every moment.*

*"I went down there, and they led me to the back. I spotted Albert in this big cell with what must'a been fifteen other guys. Some of these guys were scratching their arms, like they needed a fix. Some guys were passed out drunk. Some guys were swearing, and some were singin' weird songs, and some were just pacing or jumpin' around like caged animals. And I looked at Albert, and it was obvious he'd been drinking, too. His face was flushed, his hair was messed up, and his clothes were twisted and torn."*

*"And that was the last straw?" asked Jesus.*

*"It was. Yeah, it was. I just couldn't keep going through this week after week. He was a high school graduate. It was time for him to grow up and take some responsibility. I'd had enough. When he told me to hurry up and go pay his bail, I didn't move. He was standing on the other side of the bars, and*

*I could smell the alcohol on his breath. He looked a mess. I actually remember thinking,* <u>You're no son of mine</u>. *I turned and walked away and left him there."*

*Jesus patted Charlie on the shoulder but said nothing.*

*"I turned my face away from my own son," said Charlie, through tears. "I was his father, yet I turned my face away from him when he needed me most. I still can't believe I did that. Can you even begin to imagine the pain it would feel like to have your father turn his face from you?"*

*For a moment, Jesus looked away and seemed to be focused on something distant and ethereal. He sat transfixed as the seconds ticked by. Slowly, ever so slowly, he turned back to Charlie. "I'm sure it seemed necessary at the time," he said, as much to himself as to Charlie.*

*Charlie lowered his head. There were no words capable of assuaging his guilt and misery. "Couple of days later the judge gave Albert and his buddy a fine, which the other boy's parents paid. The boys got released. Albert slipped back home when he knew I'd be at work and my wife would be out shopping. He found two of our credit cards, went to the bank, and maxed out the day's ATM levels. He also forged my name to a check and was able to cash it. It wasn't a fortune, but it was enough to fund his exit from town. He left us a note saying that he knew we were going to spend money on Herman's college textbooks and lab fees, so he'd just take his share in cash and go out on his own."*

*"And that was the last time you ever heard from him,"* concluded Jesus.

*"Nearly five years now, like you said. Some friends of ours said they spotted Albert at a soup kitchen in Denver two years ago, or at least it was someone who looked like him. And, I got thinkin' that it was probably true. Albert was never good at managing money. He was always such a party animal. Why, most likely, he went through that money in nothin' flat."*

*"Which has always led you to believe that if he were to come home, he'd have to come by bus, the cheapest way to travel."*

*"Unless he hitchhiked. But if he looked as bad as our friends described him, I don't think anyone would stop to give him a lift. What I keep hopin' is that...."*

Suddenly, a booming voice cut short Charlie's sentence. *"Dad! Yep, I thought I'd find you here."*

Momentarily disoriented, Charlie swiveled to the right and squinted. In front of him stood a man in tan slacks, a blue blazer, and a white shirt with an expensive silk tie. Diamond studs flashed from his gold cufflinks, and his large ring was encrusted with emeralds.

*"Herman? What are you doing here?"* Charlie half-rose, but Jesus placed a hand on his forearm and kept him seated.

Herman tapped the screen of his smartphone, looking both disgusted and impatient. *"I'm here to bring you home. It's time to end this charade. My car's outside."*

"No . . . no, I can't leave yet," said Charlie. "There's gonna be two more buses before...."

"Why do you do this to yourself, Dad? Albert is dead to us. He's never coming back. I'd bet money he probably overdosed and was buried in a potter's field in some place we've never heard of."

"You'd lose that bet," said Jesus flatly.

Herman stared at the stranger. "And you would be?"

"A hand. An ear," said Jesus. "Just a friend of your dad's. And of yours."

"Of mine? I've never met you before in my life. If you need a lift, we can drop you off on our way home. I appreciate you sitting with my dad, but we're leaving this place. Come on, Dad. I need to get you home."

At that moment the Midnight Special pulled into the terminal, and Charlie bolted upright. "I ain't goin' nowhere till I see who gets off that bus." He advanced to the unloading zone and began to scrutinize the disembarking passengers. Although he kept back, he studied each person meticulously, not wanting unfamiliar dress or mannerisms or behavior to prevent him from recognizing his dear Albert.

First came the bus driver, next, a retired couple helping to support each other as they traversed the steep steps, then a mother carrying an infant and leading a toddler, then three young sailors in dress whites, then a young woman chewing gum and bobbing her head to the music coming through her *earbuds, then a college student wearing a letterman's jacket. And then...and then...could it be...?*

*Charlie moved cautiously forward. Ten feet away from him stood a hunched-back young man attired in a grungy military jacket and torn blue jeans. The fellow's hair was long, stringy, and matted. He was unshaven. His hands were shaking, and he had a nervous twitch to his head. He coughed several times, as though he were battling a cold, or perhaps even pneumonia. He was rail thin, his shirt and pants hanging on him as though he were a little boy playing dress-up with daddy's clothes. Charlie noticed that the young man wore no shoes and his socks had holes.*

*Almost staggering, Charlie advanced, opening his arms as he moved. "Albert," he breathed softly. Then louder, "Albert! Albert, I'm here, Son."*

*Albert tried to focus, but he seemed disoriented. Suddenly, however, recognition became obvious. "Pa!" he said, in true amazement. "Oh, Pa, it's really you. How...how did you know?"*

*Charlie closed the distance and bear-hugged his son. He squeezed and squeezed and squeezed, as though letting his boy go would cause him to disappear once more. Charlie's heart was overflowing with surprise, with joy, with praise. "Oh, my son, my son," he repeated over and over. "How I've longed for this day."*

*After a moment, he pulled back slightly and began to kiss his son's forehead, his cheeks. Then, once again, he engulfed him in his big arms. "You'll come home. We'll get you cleaned up. Your Ma, she's gonna fix all your favorite foods. Still like lamb stew? Sure, you do. Come on, let's get this filthy coat off you."*

*"Pa...I've shamed you. I got no right to...."*

*"Shhh, none of that," said Charlie, suddenly crying. "You were dead, and now you are alive again. Nothing else matters." Turning, Charlie waved Herman to come to him. Herman, wanting nothing to do with this pathetic reunion, took two steps, then halted.*

*"Get over here, Herman," demanded Charlie. "Take off your sport coat. Give it to me. Hurry!"*

*Herman's mouth fell open. "What! This coat cost me five hundred bucks. I'm not going to...."*

*Suddenly, Jesus ran forward, grabbed Herman by the coat collar, and yanked him across the platform to where his father was now holding up his brother. Jesus jerked Herman's face directly in front of Albert and held him there, proving to be much stronger than anyone might have imagined. "Look at your brother!" Jesus demanded.*

*Albert's stench made Herman nauseous, but Jesus was relentless in his grip.*

*"I said, look at him," Jesus repeated. "Is this the brother you've been jealous of all these years? Is this the brother you've told everyone you were cheated by? Where did it get him? Look closely at him. Have you really been so greatly wronged by this brother of yours?"*

*Albert let go of his father and sank to his knees. It was abundantly apparent he had not eaten for days. Jesus forced Herman onto his knees as well, and continued to hold him captive.*

*"If your brother has wronged you, he has been his own judge and jury. Look closely at him and try to tell me you've been shortchanged by comparison. He's starving. His clothes are rags. He hasn't bathed in weeks. His hair has lice. He's missing two teeth. His nose is broken. He's coughing blood. Do you hate your brother so much that you would want to inflict even more agony on him?"*

*The faces of the two brothers, now so close together, were like distorted reflections. That they had once been mirror images was obvious, but that they had now become aliens was equally obvious.*

*Herman's eyes narrowed. An expression of remembered antagonism came over him as he glared mercilessly at his ailing twin. "You squandered it all," he said, virtually hissing at Albert. "You squandered it all."*

*Albert nodded in abdication. "Yeah, yeah, every dime, you're right, and I should...."*

*"I'm not talking about the money!" snapped Herman. "I'm talking about your gifts. We were twins, but you were the one who was naturally coordinated...the big sports star who didn't even have to practice...the swimmer, the diver, the runner, the jumper. You were the funny one, too. Everyone*

*always wanted to be around you. Mr. Life-of-the-Party, my dear brother Albert."*

*Albert looked truly confused. "But you...you were the brains. Honor roll and scholarships. I hated being in your shadow. I tried. I really tried, but I could never get the grades you always got. It was so simple for you."*

*"Simple? It wasn't simple. I was up all night doing extra-credit assignments, memorizing dates and mathematical formulas and chemical compounds. It was the only way I could stay even with you in some arena. You hated being in my shadow? How'd you like to be the kid who got picked last for every event, while your brother always got picked first? Try living with that!"*

*There was a heavy silence, then Charlie finally said, "You know what happened? You can see it, can't ya? You boys wanted to be each other. All these years of feeling hatred toward each other, but you were each other's biggest fans. Albert wanted to be Herman, and Herman wanted to be Albert. And look where it got you, boys. All these years, you could have been helpin' each other. Instead, you're still livin' with the hate."*

*Jesus released his grip on Herman. "Look closely at each other," he said. "You've got fine clothes, Herman, but you'll never be dressed as elegantly as even the lilies of the field. And on the inside, your soul is as destitute as the wretchedness of your brother."*

*Herman, still kneeling on the dirty platform, blinked for a moment and then stared at Jesus. He seemed unaware that his white shirt had come untucked and his silk tie hung askew.*

*Jesus reached out to Albert and gently lifted his chin. "And you, Albert, have independence and defiance, but your life is shallow and destructive. As I see it, you each are half a man. Together, you just might make something whole out of each other."*

*Albert coughed several times, then raised one hand. "I'm sorry, Pa. And I'm sorry, Herm. I've made a lot of mistakes. If you'll let me come back, I'll do anything you want. I'll work in the garden...wash the cars...mow the lawn..."*

*Herman put an unsteady finger to his brother's lips. "That's all right," he said gruffly. "Let me worry about all that."*

*"What?" asked Albert, clearly shocked.*

*Herman glanced up at Jesus and then back to his brother. "I see it now. You just need to rebuild your strength. I've been enjoying the good life all the years you've been gone. Now, it's your turn."*

*Herman stood and shrugged off his coat and placed it around his brother's shoulders. He pulled the ring off his finger and pushed it onto his brother's finger. He leaned his brother slightly backward and lifted his feet. He slipped off his pair of Gucci shoes and put them on Albert.*

*Jesus looked at Charlie. "Rejoice," he said, "for today both of your sons have come home."*

## LIVING EXPANSIVELY, NOT DEFENSIVELY

Charles Kettering, the engineering genius who developed General Motors, once said, "We have come to fear failure too much. Failure is nothing more than the practice essential to success."

Whereas most people would agree with him in theory, they still would not embrace this idea of increasing the number of failures in their lives as a way of advancing themselves. It is human nature to fear failure.

Remember when Moses asked God, "What if they will not believe me or listen to what I say?" (Exodus 4:1). And how about Gideon, who gulped and said, "How can I do that, Lord?" These men, like others, feared personal failure even though they *knew God was on their side.*

In my work as college professor, church deacon, and business consultant, I have encountered endless numbers of people who have experienced a major failure in their lives that has caused them to live *defensively* rather than *expansively.* "Burn me once, shame on you; burn me twice, shame on me" became their philosophy. Because of this cautious mindset, they never reached their full potential either as professionals in their line of work or as human beings.

When I try to encourage such people to push themselves to new heights, they immediately counter with a story of a tragic event in their lives. Their failures run the gamut of human experiences: a bankrupt business, marital unfaithfulness, dismissal from a good job, a bad investment, a broken friendship, a public embarrassment, a lost election, or even a bad dating relationship.

Ironically, if I ask these people to tell me the names of people in the Bible whom they greatly admire, they usually mention people who were incredible failures at some point in their lives. Moses lost his temper; David stole another man's wife; Peter denied Christ three times. The list is long. No person of success or stature is without a past strewn with mistakes, judgment errors, and outright failures. Such setbacks are, indeed, "the practice essential to success."

If you find yourself burdened with memories of past failures as you begin a new endeavor, make an effort to take steps to relieve yourself of these burdens. The Bible offers ways to go about this.

***See things with a different perspective.*** Romans 8:28 says, "In all things God works for the good of those who love him." This may be hard to see at the moment, but with faith, you can perceive even negative events as positive steps in your life.

I once applied to the creative writing program of a prestigious graduate school in Michigan. My application was denied. I failed to get admitted because my portfolio was over-balanced with works of journalism. This was a career setback for me, as well as a blow to my ego. However, it forced me to reevaluate my development as writer. I began to study the craft of fiction writing. Two years later I was admitted to a graduate writing program in Indiana, where I completed my PhD and subsequently wrote six successful novels. My earlier failure led to a greater success later on.

***Offer forgiveness to those who may have caused failure in your life.*** Ephesians 4:32 says, "Be kind and compassionate to one another, forgiving each other, just as in Christ God forgave you." Admittedly, at times in life your failures are not your fault. An unscrupulous partner may have stolen company funds, leading to your company's bankruptcy. A drunken driver may have rear-ended your car, causing you to miss a job interview and, thus, a job. God sees all. His justice is pure. His scales are still in balance.

I once loaned several hundred dollars to a man who was attending our church and was between jobs. He promised to pay me back as soon as he found work. In time, he became a successful car salesman, but he ignored my calls and letters asking for the repayments of the loan. He later moved out of state to work at a larger dealership.

When I told my wife I had made an error of judgment and had lost our money, she said, "We can get past this. He, however, will have to live with it the rest of his life. His punishment is worse than our loss." Once I saw it from her perspective, I forgave the man, felt sorry for him, and I moved forward with my life.

**Provide continual affirmation to others who are recovering from failure.** Moses told Joshua, "Be strong and courageous," (Deut. 31:23).

It has been said that a joy shared with someone else is doubled, and a burden shared is cut in half. Interestingly, by making yourself a cheerleader for someone whose self-esteem has been shattered, you become a cheerleader for yourself, too.

I recall a summer in which a book I had written turned out to be ahead of its time. It came across as "over the top" for several critics who gave it scathing reviews. I had worked more than two years researching and writing that book, so having it lambasted was very disheartening.

To get my mind off of it, I called a friend of mine who had just lost a great deal of money in a failed franchise effort. I spent thirty minutes on the phone telling him how much I admired his entrepreneurial drive and how I was confident he would find a new opportunity soon that would be successful. It lifted my friend's spirits and, in the process, got my mind on more positive thoughts. By helping others, we also help ourselves.

As you take on any new challenge, you can be like an Olympic runner who trains with lead weights strapped around her ankles. Later, when she enters the race free of burdens, she feels as though she can run forever. You can be equally strong emotionally and spiritually if you will shed your excess burdens of past failures. Accept the freedom. Make it a new opportunity for success.

## Key Points Found in Section 7

1. Everyone, including great heroes of the Bible, has faced some sort of failure in life.

2. Failure can be beneficial if it is used as a learning experience.

3. God can use all things—even our failures—for good if we yield our lives to him.

4. Forgiving those who have wronged us is a positive step in self-restoration.

5. Offering encouragement to those facing failure blesses them and also you.

6. Carrying the guilt and anger regarding past failures is like burdening yourself with lead weights. Release them, and you'll be able to run again.

*Beau Asbury was almost ready to hit "send" on his e-mail to Jesus when the man himself walked into the company's security booth.*

*"Morning, Beau. How's it going?"*

*Beau froze, stared at Jesus for ten seconds, turned down the volume of the R&B song playing in the background, and said, "How do you always do that? Just as I'm about to send you a message or call you on the phone, you walk in here. Are you psychic or something? That's like the fifth or sixth time that's happened."*

*"Just observant," said Jesus. "You didn't clock out this morning. Made me want to see what you were up to."*

*Beau nodded slightly, weighed that a second or two, then shrugged it off. "Yeah, well, I've got something here I need your take on, Boss. I mean, I can't say we've got a hardened criminal on our hands, but it's also not like we can let this slide."*

*Jesus pulled a chair up to where Beau was seated in front of a panel of four security monitors. "Explain."*

*"Okay, this is a new wrinkle. I've been working security here for about a year, and I put in five years doing security for Wellspring Industries before that. Then there's my twenty years with the Marines. I've caught thieves, embezzlers,*

*smugglers, hijackers, con artists, and shysters of every sort. But what I'm about to show you is one for the books. We've got ourselves someone who's entering our main manufacturing building every night and cleaning up the place."*

Jesus smiled knowingly. *"You have some footage to show me?"*

*"Indeed, I do, and if you can figure out what's going on, then maybe I'll know whether to call the cops or add this woman to the payroll."* Beau cued up a video and said, *"Let's go back four nights when she first came in. It's a little grainy, but you can see a dark figure crawling through a window right here. Her face is covered, so maybe she knew there were security cameras. Maybe not, however, since she came back the next three nights. Anyway, watch what she does."*

The thin, black woman on the screen could be seen removing a burlap sack from over her shoulder. Methodically, she picked up scraps of wood and put them into the sack. She worked quickly and efficiently until the bag was quite full. Then, after looking around furtively to make sure no one was in the room, she made her way back to the window, crawled outside, and was gone.

Beau pause the video. *"I won't waste your time showing you recordings of the other three nights because they're pretty much identical. It's like reverse-Santa Claus. She comes in with a sack, fills it, and then leaves. But she fills it with scrap. She's picking up the shaved-off chips our carpenters let fall to the floor when they're lathing rocking chairs and baby cribs. A maintenance crew arrives at five in the morning to sweep up all the splinters and woodchips so the area will be clean and safe when the workers show up at seven. She's got most of their work done for them, though."*

*Jesus looked at the screen. He smiled. "Maybe you were on to something when you suggested adding her to the payroll."*

*"And there's something else," said Beau. "And try not to laugh at me when I tell you this because I already know it's weird." He sat for a moment trying to form his words.*

*"You think you may know this woman," said Jesus.*

*Beau flinched. Then he glared. "You creep me out when you do stuff like that. I used to think my mom had eyes in the back of her head, but you've got her beat, no contest. How do you...?"*

*"What makes you think you might know her?"*

*Beau lifted his shoulders. "Don't know exactly. From the way she moves, she appears young, probably mid-twenties. Could be something about her hair, her size, the way she carries herself. At first I thought maybe she reminded me of someone on TV or in a movie I'd seen, but no one's come to mind. I've replayed the footage, and the more I watch her, the more I have this gut feeling I know her. However, putting that aside, what really bugs me is trying to figure out what in blazes she's doing with that wood."*

*"Just that," said Jesus.*

146

*Beau waited a moment. "Just what?"*

*"Figure it out. What do our clean-up people do with all the wood chips they gather every morning?"*

*"It gets recycled. It's taken to the grinder, it gets pulverized into sawdust, and then it's force-blown into our furnace. We use it as a power source."*

*"So, if we turn it into blazes, what do you think this woman is doing with it?"*

*Beau pondered that a moment and said, "She looks like a street person. My guess is she's burning it to keep warm. She's homeless, isn't she? She's no thief. She's just taking what she thinks we'll throw away anyway, and she's using it to keep warm. Wow, how pathetic is that? Sad."*

*Jesus stood. "How do you think I want you to handle this, Beau?"*

*Beau almost chuckled. "I know exactly what you're gonna say." He pointed to the screen. "Tonight, make sure they leave bigger pieces of scrap wood on the floor."*

*It was almost midnight when the woman showed up again. Beau, dressed in all black, crouched in the alley outside the factory. He knew his dark skin would blend into the shadows as he watched her pull open the window and crawl inside. Within twenty minutes the woman reemerged. Beau*

*let her regain the sidewalk, then began to follow her. It wasn't safe for a woman to be walking the streets of a large city alone in the dead of night, and this woman seemed to be acutely aware of that. She took pains to keep to the shadows, pausing now and then as if to discern if anyone were approaching. Beau was no stranger to surveillance, so he stalked the woman undetected.*

*It didn't surprise Beau that the path the woman followed led toward a skid row section of town. Beau knew that cops basically ignored the area populated by derelicts, winos, and endless numbers of homeless folks who spent their days on the streets begging. Some of these people were undocumented immigrants. Some were drifters or day workers. Most were loners, but others had friends or family who clustered with them, eking out an existence as best they could collectively.*

*Stealthily, Beau wound his way through a maze of makeshift shanties cobbled together from refrigerator crates, cardboard boxes, and scraps of lumber. At last the woman with the sack stopped in front of a lean-to of what appeared to be a hodge-podge of concrete blocks, broken bricks, and piled broken furniture covered by wire mesh and old rugs. Feeble smoke rose from a large oil drum in front of the lean-to. Several women of various ages, various ethnicities, all gaunt and dirty, were gathered around, holding their hands over a waning fire.*

*"Stand back," said the woman with the sack. "Let me feed the fire. The scraps are larger tonight. We'll be warmer*

*for a longer time." She tossed in several chunks of wood, then picked up a blackened metal rod and stirred the coals. A flame arose, and the other women murmured joy and approval as they inched back closer to the warmth.*

*"Thank you, daughter," said one older woman. "I have no husband, no sons, no brothers, yet you care for me. I would have perished by now, had it not been for you."*

*"Have you eaten?" asked the young woman.*

*"Enough to get by," was the reply. "I made it to the soup kitchen at noon. One good meal each day is enough to sustain this wisp of a body."*

*Beau caught his breath in the darkness, stunned by his discovery. This older woman...this young woman...he knew them! His youngest cousin Kelly had gone to the Dominican Republic years ago with the Peace Corps. He'd married a girl there—Ruthella. Beau had flown down for the wedding. But after Kelly died in a plane crash, and Kelly's mother—Beau's aunt—had gone down to live with Ruthella, Beau had lost track of that part of the family. This aging woman, now living in abject poverty, was his Aunt Naomi. Even though she'd lost a lot of weight and no longer wore her cherished acrylic nails or intricate cornrows, he'd know her anywhere. When had she come back to America, and how in the world had she wound up living in such desperation? This was outrageous!*

*His immediate impulse was to step out and reveal himself. But then he hesitated. Would he frighten them? Would* he confuse them? Surely they would be happy to see a long lost relative. But then, maybe they'd be embarrassed, ashamed of their circumstances. And, even if they were pleased to see him, what then? He lived in a mid-sized apartment. He had only a modest savings. What could he do for them?

He realized this would take some time and contemplation. Quietly, he eased away from the campsite and made his way back to the factory.

As he finished the night shift, Beau pondered his options regarding his aunt and his cousin's widow. Having never married and now in his early forties, he hadn't had to worry about anyone except himself. He'd never earned a fortune, although he was free of debt and living comfortably. But to help care for two other people? That would be a financial challenge. Maybe he should ask the Boss for advice. Good thought. Yeah, the Boss always had a way of seeing things clearly and wisely.

Beau whirled his chair around and was about to pull the e-mail address of Jesus from his address file when an electronic message arrived addressed to him: <u>Please come to my office before leaving today. J.</u>

Beau gawked at the screen, then shook his head ever so slightly. "How does he always know...?"

When Beau arrived outside the office, Martha waved him to a seat. Already waiting were two other men: Steve Summers, who did something with overseas sales, and Justin

*Charton, who helped coordinate the fleet of delivery trucks. Being involved in security, Beau knew them, of course, but he seldom actually crossed paths with either man. They all nodded silent greetings.*

*The door opened, and Jesus invited the men inside. He motioned them to take the three chairs flanking his desk. "You three men have now been with our company one year," Jesus began, seating himself behind the desk. "You came in with different levels of training and experience, so I set different expectations for you. Today is assessment day."*

*Beau had known that the company held year-end reviews, but he thought they took place in summer. This seemed to be something different. Was he in some kind of trouble?*

*"Steve, I tasked you with opening our new distribution centers in the Middle East. I authorized a million dollars for you to use as you saw fit. I've followed your dealings and operations. You've worked very hard. You've doubled that million to two million. That pleases me because it will allow us to do good work in a lot of new places, helping a lot of needy people."*

*"Thank you, sir. I'll confess to you, though, I took a few risks, and I also made a couple of really bad decisions. But, in the end it has panned out pretty well for us. I really enjoy working here. I wanted to please you."*

*Jesus smiled. "And you have. So much so, in fact, I'm doubling your budget to two million, and I'm giving you a 20 percent raise effective this week."*

*Steve's jaw dropped.*

*Beau reached over, slapped him on the shoulder, and said, "Congratulations, man. Well done!"*

*Steve began to express his appreciation and gratitude, but Jesus lifted a hand and shifted slightly. "And you, Beau. Judas hired you to create a security system for our plant and warehouses. He gave you a budget of half a million dollars. You installed most of the electronic systems yourself. You found ways to cut costs by buying surplus military equipment. You also reduced our overhead by discovering how several of our outside vendors were taking unfair advantage of us. You used only half of your budget and saved us a quarter of a million dollars."*

*Beau shrugged, feeling somewhat self-conscious. "If you can't feel secure with your own security people...."*

*"I'm expanding your responsibilities, Beau. You're now also going to be director of security for our new overseas distribution centers. You can put your head together with Steve, here, about that. He can give you the details about locations, layouts, and related matters. Oh, and you're getting a 20 percent raise, too. I have a feeling it'll come in handy just now. Ever thought about getting married?"*

*"Married?" Beau almost yelped. "Me?"*

*"Just a thought," said Jesus.*

*He again shifted slightly and faced Justin Charton. "Justin, you've had a year with us, too. You came highly recommended. I assigned an expense account to your office of a hundred thousand dollars. I asked you to streamline the delivery operation, upgrade the loading equipment, train the drivers better, and make the fleet safer for transporting goods. I can't see where you've done anything along those lines."*

*Justin straightened in his chair. "Well, I've come to work every day, sir. I've never missed a single day, no, not one day. I've tried to encourage the men, and I've checked some of the equipment myself. Best of all, I haven't spent even one penny of that hundred thousand dollars you authorized me to use. You still have it all, right there in the account. All of it."*

*"If I'd wanted to let it sit idle, I wouldn't have needed to turn it over to you, would I?"*

*Justin squirmed slightly. "But…uh, I saw how well this company was running, sir, and I figured out quickly that you…well, that you wouldn't be happy if I came up with a loss at the end of the year. So, I was…I was…<u>conservative</u>."*

*"I never ordered you to bat a thousand. Business requires some experiments, some challenges. You don't always succeed, but you have to make the effort. 'Not losing' is not the same as winning. You have to be a good steward of everything given to you—money, work, health…." He paused and shifted his gaze to Beau. "…even family."*

*Beau's eyes narrowed. <u>Could he possibly…?</u>*

*"Well, I can certainly give it a better shot this next year," proclaimed Justin, as if trying to sound very self-assured.*

*"No, this is it. I'm letting you go," said Jesus. "I've been lenient, but now I need someone in that position who will do right by those workers."*

*Justin half-rose from his chair. "But I planned to work here my entire life."*

*Jesus looked at him solemnly. "Not everyone who says to me, 'Boss, Boss' qualifies for the 401(k) plan. I wish you well." He arose, indicating the meeting was over.*

*As Beau left the office and walked slowly to his truck, he pondered how a 20 percent raise would change his life. Maybe he could begin with a few personal improvements. Dye some of that graying hair? Join a gym and shed some of that middle-age spread he'd picked up since leaving the Corps? Well, yeah, things like that were options, but he had something else to do first.*

*He drove to the parking lot of the soup kitchen nearest where his aunt and Ruthella had thrown together their lean-to. He'd overheard his aunt say she'd visited a soup kitchen, so this would be the most likely one. It opened at noon, so if Aunt Naomi followed routine, she would show up then.*

*Beau smiled, set the alarm on his cell phone for 11:45 a.m., and then leaned back his seat. Two decades in the Marines had conditioned him to sleep in any locale, under any conditions, for any specific length of time. He was out almost instantly.*

*In what seemed like no time, his phone alarm beeped. At the same time there came a rapping on the passenger's side window of his truck.*

*"Beauregard! Beauregard! Unlock this door!"*

*Beau bolted upright, shook his head to clear the cobwebs, and squinted at the window. It was his Aunt Naomi. He hadn't found her, she'd found him. He scrambled to lean over and unlock and open the door. Then he extended a hand and pulled the older lady inside.*

*"Aunt Naomi," he said. "You recognized me?" He opened his arms in welcome.*

*Naomi accepted his embrace. "Recognized you? Oh, dear, sweet Beauregard, I've been stalking you for more than a month. You're the only relative I have left on this planet, but I wasn't sure if you'd be happy to see an old broken-down crone like me. When I saw you sleeping in this truck, it took me two seconds to guess you were hunting me, too. You have no idea how happy I am to see you."*

*"What happened, Auntie? The last time I heard about you, you'd moved to the island to live with Kelly and Ruthella. I thought you'd be a grandmother by now, enjoying a life in the tropics."*

*Naomi dropped her face into her hands. "It all went so terribly wrong. First, Kelly left on that assignment and died in the plane crash. Then our home was destroyed in an earthquake. We lost everything. Back here in the States, I'd left my house with a rental company, but when the economy crashed, the house went into foreclosure. I had to sell a half interest of it to the rental brokers just so I wouldn't lose it. And all the rent started going for my share of the mortgage, so I now have no income, but I can't live in the home either."*

*"How'd you manage to get back to the States?"*

*Naomi lifted her face, and tears spilled down her cheeks. "That's the most shameful part of it all," she confessed. "Ruthie, my lovely daughter-in-law, applied for a green card. She speaks English, Spanish, and French. She agreed to come to this country and work for six years as an au pair for a family with two daughters. The family made her sign a ridiculous contract, but it provided airfare for the two of us. They treat her like a slave. They make her wash dishes, do the shopping and laundry, care for the girls, clean the house—and for no wages. They say she has to work off the up-front expenses she cost them, plus interest. According to the agreement, if they say they aren't satisfied with her, they can send her back."*

*"Back to the island?"*

*"She's still not a US citizen," said Naomi. "We're living in a hovel, existing on what scraps of food she can bring home after preparing the evening meal for the family." She squeezed her bony hands together. "I wasn't sure you even still lived in the area. I knew you'd been in the military, traveling a lot. But Ruthie found your name in the phonebook, and she discovered where you worked. Found out you were on the night shift doing something. But once she got there, she was just too embarrassed to go in and beg from you."*

*"So* <u>*that's*</u> *how she found out about our factory," Beau mused softly.*

*"I've come by your business a couple of times, to get a glimpse of you, but somehow I just couldn't...."*

*Beau reached over and turned the ignition. "Buckle your seatbelt, Auntie. We're going to a nice restaurant for lunch together, then we're going to get you some new clothes. After that, I'm taking you to my apartment, where you can get cleaned up and start sleeping in a bed."*

*"But...what about my Ruthie?"*

*"Don't worry. I know some people. Good people, Auntie. They'll be able to help us."*

*Matt Feingold came back into his office. Beau looked at him questioningly.*

*"Okay, I called in a few favors," said Matt. "In my days as an IRS auditor I got to know a lot of bankers and real estate agents. They pulled some records. Here's the deal. You're aunt's house went underwater—you know, below market value—so that she owed more on the mortgage security than the house had in balancing equity. It's still in her name for the time being, but she has only three more months to put up the needed equity balance. Otherwise, her new 'partners' can exercise a clause allowing them to secure the property by direct*

purchase. Naturally, it will be at far below the price she and her late husband originally paid for the place."

"Is it hopeless?" asked Beau.

"Depends," said Matt. "You have a perfect credit record and a military pension and a steady job. If you wanted to assume the responsibility, you could take out a private loan, have your aunt deed the property over to you, and you could pull a switcheroo on the loan sharks. You could buy the property at the newly reduced rate, pay them off at the discount price, and you'd own the place outright."

Beau swallowed hard. "What…what would that set me back?"

Matt quoted a figure. "But it would be a good deal. The house is actually worth twice that much—or it will be when prices start to climb again. Which they always do sooner or later with real estate. Plus, you wouldn't have to pay rent any longer, you'd also get tax credits on your mortgage interest, and you'd have a place for your aunt and her daughter-in-law to live comfortably. I can arrange the paperwork, if you want to do this."

"Three months, eh?" said Beau. "Yeah, yeah, let me give this some thought. Hey, man, I can't thank you enough for helping me like this."

Matt smiled. "Word came down to me that you're to be given a nice raise. That might help make the decision a little easier."

"Yeah, well, on the house deal maybe," said Beau, "but I still don't know what to do about that mess Ruthie got herself into. I don't want to see her slaving away for that family any longer, but I don't want them to deport her either."

"Where is she now?" asked Matt.

"My place. My aunt and I picked her up after work, took her shopping, and then brought her home. I left the two of them there while I came to meet with you. I appreciate you staying after hours to help me like this. I didn't know who else to turn to...you know, someone with a business background. Thanks again."

Beau rose, started to leave, then paused. Deep in thought, he turned back to Matt. "Can I ask you something personal? Have you ever found yourself in a situation like this? I mean, you know, having to make a decision that will radically alter what you do, how you'll live, what your future will be?"

"Just once," said Matt. "I took the leap of faith. Best thing that ever happened to me."

"Really?" said Beau. "You mean that?" He stood motionless, as though assessing his past and projecting his future. Finally, in a small voice he said, "You know, I think I'm gonna take you up on that offer to help me with the loans and the home purchase."

By the time Beau finally made it back to his apartment, it was very late. He'd taken a personal business day so his night *shift would be covered and he and Matt would have time to complete the paperwork needed for his loans and purchases. The apartment was dark and soundless. He entered quietly. He'd told the women to take his bedroom, so without even bothering to undress, he just stretched out on the couch and threw an afghan over himself.*

*Around three in the morning Beau shifted on the couch and his leg came into contact with something warm and soft. His nostrils detected a pleasant fragrance in the air. He reached for the lamp and turned it on. Lying at the foot of the couch was Ruthella, arrayed in a lovely pink kimono-styled wraparound. Her face glowed softly in the lamplight.*

*"Ruthie," he said. "You all right, kiddo?"*

*She shook her head. "No. I am lonely and sad and tired. More than anything, I am unfulfilled. I don't wish to continue this way."*

*Beau sat up. "Hey, we'll think of something," he whispered. "Looks like we're gonna get a house. I started the paperwork today. That's a start, right?"*

*Ruthella looked directly into Beau's eyes. "I have watched you from afar, Beau. And now I've been with you up close. Naomi has told me how fine a man you are. She's right. I have instinct about such things." She moved slightly closer to him. "I don't want just a house. I want a home. I want love and purpose and a family once again. Beau, will you marry me and make it possible for me to stay in the United States with you?"*

*Beau went numb for a moment.* <u>*Huh? Say wha-?*</u> *Slowly, he pinched himself. Ouch! No, it wasn't a dream. Insane as it might seem, indeed, this gorgeous, intelligent, sensitive, twenty-six-year-old young woman had just asked him to marry her.*

*Beau had been in combat, he had confronted criminals, and he had dealt with every kind of situation a man with his responsibilities could be confronted with. But never in his life had he ever experienced exhilaration. Until now.*

*He stared long and intently at Ruthie. "First thing tomorrow, I'm buying you out of that contract," he vowed.*

*Ruthie crawled over him, turned out the lamp, and lay contentedly against his chest.*

## Section *8*

## Gaining Wisdom: Every Person Is Self-Educated

My late father, L. Edward Hensley, built three optical companies in his lifetime, owned real estate, and served on the optician advisory board of Ferris State University. That's not bad for a fellow who had to quit school after eighth grade, enlisted in the Navy at age seventeen during World War II, and later completed a night-school optician's certificate while caring for a wife and kids.

How'd he do it? Pragmatism. Dreams and goals. Sweat equity. Discipline. Determination. Ambition. Taking some risks. Discovering the ground floor in his career field and getting in on it early (contact lenses in 1958). Self-study. Charisma. Social connections. Learning from mistakes. Never forgetting to laugh. Playing golf.

As for me, I have a lot of formal education. Yet, I discovered early in life that my father's common sense, his basic logic, and his clear analysis of what life was really all about could serve as my measuring stick against which I could compare everything else I was taught. My father had the ability to crystallize wisdom into succinct phrases. Sometimes they would be lessons I already knew but needed to be reminded of. Other times they would be completely new insights. Either way, they were solid.

In regard to education, I turned to my father many times. In 1966, when it came time to make important decisions about my future education, I sought my father's advice. Many of my graduating friends were going off to large state universities. My father surprised me by calling that a waste of time and money.

"But the University of Michigan, where my friend Larry is going, has one of the finest accounting programs in the country," I argued. "And Vanderbilt, where my friend Mike is going, is renowned for its pre-law program. And Purdue, where Margie is going, is famous for its veterinary science program."

My dad smiled and asked, "And they all think that by showing up on a specific piece of property—a designated college—it will ensure that they will become highly educated and on their way to a lifetime of success?"

I shrugged. "Well, those schools have great facilities and famous professors and huge libraries. That'll give my friends some real advantages."

"No, it won't," said my father. "It will just cost them a lot of money they will have to borrow and then take years to pay back."

I looked at him almost sympathetically, knowing that since he had never gone to college, he probably didn't have the foggiest idea about what comprised a college education. Of course, in this, as with many other things regarding my father, I was totally wrong. The man knew how to "look into things."

"Let me ask you a few questions," my father said. "If you were to live here at home—eating your mother's cooking and sleeping in your own bed—while driving back and forth to community college, would your rest and nutrition be anything less than what you might experience if you ate in a university cafeteria and slept in a crowded dormitory?"

I was forced to admit, "Well, I'm sure mom's cooking is probably a lot tastier than mass-produced cafeteria food. And my room here is quiet and private, and my bed is comfortable. Okay, sure, I guess I'd actually be better off on those two points."

"All right," he continued, "and what about those huge university libraries you referred to? Is there virtually any book in America that you could not obtain via interlibrary loan through the community college?"

I considered that, then said, "Well, yeah, actually most of the university libraries are connected, and they exchange books and other references materials just for the asking. So, sure, I guess I could borrow and use any of the books found in any major university library."

He nodded. "And regarding the famous professors you mentioned at these large universities...." He paused for effect. "That's not as big a deal as you may think. I know a little about that. For one thing, a lot of those lecture hall presentations are filled with as many as three hundred students, with very little time for asking questions, much less developing a personal relationship with the professor. Most students have to settle for appointments with graduate assistants. And if the professors are tenured, they sometimes don't even show up for all the lectures. They'll have underlings cover for them. They're often too involved in research projects or TV appearances or guest speaking engagements elsewhere. However, at our community college, your professors will have regular office hours, their class sizes will be much smaller so they'll know their students, and they'll do their own teaching. To me, that seems much more productive."

"But what about the prestige of graduating from a Big Ten school or an Ivy League university?" I pressed. "Doesn't that open a lot of doors when you go looking for a job?"

My dad smiled. "When I was in basic training with all the other men, do you think the drill instructor cared two cents whether a man was a high school dropout or a graduate of Cornell? Trust me, he didn't. Each man had to do his own push-ups, reach his own marksmanship qualifications, master his own first-aid skills, and swim his own laps. If you did the work well, you passed. If you didn't, you were made to do it over and over until you finally got it right. Prestigious degrees had nothing to do with it."

I started to interrupt, but he was on a roll.

"And how about sports?" he added. "Look at the NFL and, sure, you'll find players who attended some prestigious colleges and played football for Notre Dame and Ohio State University. But you'll also find kids from Division Two schools and some even straight out of high school. It's their skill at playing the game that counts, not what school they attended."

I weighed that a moment. I could see that on certain "playing fields" a degree from a hotshot college might not count for anything. Still....

## Every Person Is Self-Educated

"Let me explain something I learned a long time ago," my father continued, sensing he had not completely convinced me. "In the final analysis, every person is self-educated. If you go to Harvard University and cut classes, party every weekend, and then cram just before finals so you can jam enough facts in your head to squeak by an exam, you might wind up with a degree, but you sure as heck won't have an education. However, if you go to our local Delta Community College and you stay current with your homework, read your textbooks carefully, ask pertinent questions, and master the latest information in your field, you'll graduate with experience, knowledge, and capabilities. Once in the working world, you will mop the floor with any Harvard grad who just played at college."

My dad motioned to an old family photo hanging on the wall.

"When I was a kid in Tennessee, I got up before dawn to do chores on the farm," he explained. "I then went to school, came home, did more chores. In the summertime I worked in the cotton fields. I would be sweating in a delta, picking cotton for hours on end, and I'd look up and see people off at a distance driving their nice cars on the highway. I told my friends that one day I'd own a fine car, too. They laughed. They knew that we'd all be leaving school after eighth grade and be expected to do field labor or factory work for the rest of our lives. High school wasn't for 'our kind.' But I had already figured out that you didn't have to be in school in order to become educated."

He opened a couple of soft drinks and handed me one. I sipped mine as he continued.

"After eighth grade I wrote to my older cousin, who was a bank guard in Detroit. I told him I wanted to get a job and also learn a trade. He sent me the money to come to Detroit, and he got me a job running a newsstand inside the bank where he worked. I was only fifteen, but I worked nine hours a day, delivering papers to all the offices on the nineteen floors of that bank building. When I wasn't delivering papers, I was back at the newsstand selling candy bars, cigarettes, chewing gum, magazines, shoe polish, ink pens, soda pop, and paperback novels. I got a small hourly salary and a commission, so I was a hustler at selling.

"At nights, I would grab a couple of hot dogs at a Coney stand and then race off to evening classes at Wilbur Wright Trade School. This was the 1940s, so they taught me how to grind lenses for prescription eyeglasses and fit the lenses into frames. I finished the apprenticeship program and then became a journeyman. After class I would go home and read books from the Detroit Public Library. I'd be up until midnight reading novels by Hemingway, books on history and geography, and some texts on basic science. I'd then sleep awhile, get a quick breakfast, and be back at the newsstand by 6:45 each morning."

"How did you know what books to read if you didn't have a teacher?" I asked.

"I *did* have teachers," he said. "I'd ask the librarians to direct me to what was best to read in any area I was trying to gain knowledge in. Librarians are always eager to help sincere patrons. And when I'd deliver the newspapers to attorneys, insurance executives, and accountants, I'd ask them to recommend business books they felt would be helpful, and they always had good suggestions. Teachers are always available…you can always find free books. If you don't gain an education in America, it's your own fault."

"You're saying you gained as much education by studying on your own as you would have if you'd actually gone to high school?" I challenged him.

"What I'm saying," he counterpointed, "is that I was getting a whole lot more education than my friends who stayed in Tennessee and continued to pick cotton. Maybe going to high school instead of trade school would have expanded my education in ways I wasn't experiencing back then. But, then again, maybe not. A lot of kids stay in school because it's expected of them. That wasn't the case with me. I went to trade school to master a skill that would earn me a better income than sweating fourteen hours a day in a cotton field. However, I was also motivated to learn a variety of other subjects."

### The Goal Is a Real Education

I lifted a hand. "But be honest, Dad. You couldn't get into college with a trade school optician's certificate. You had to have a high school diploma."

"You're missing the point," he responded. "I never had a goal of going to college. I had a goal only of *becoming educated*. That's the only thing that counts in life, son. It all comes down to *what you know, what you can do,* and *how well* you can do it."

"But your approach seems like it was all hodgepodge," I argued. "Some trade school classes…some random personal readings…a little mentoring from a few office executives…."

He smiled and responded, "That's because you think only linearly. When you attended high school, you were made to follow sequences that best suited the organization of the school. To that end, you read American literature in freshman English class. The next year you read British literature. One year you did geometry, the next year algebra. But, as for me, I was never bound by such constraints. I was open to all learning, at all times, in all places, from all people."

"Meaning what?" I asked.

"*Meaning,*" he explained, "that just because I was studying physics and light refraction and wave theory as part of my optician's training at night, it didn't prevent me from talking with an attorney in the bank building the next day about a book I'd been reading on buying real estate. Similarly, just because I enjoyed reading novels late at night by Mark Twain and John Steinbeck, it didn't mean I couldn't go with my cousin on Saturday afternoons to the firing range to learn to shoot his pistol. What seems like a 'hodgepodge' of learning to you was a *cornucopia* of learning to me. People who want to advance in life will take every opportunity to gain new knowledge. They don't worry about it needing to be in a set curriculum or agenda. They become the deans of their own institutions of higher learning. They self-educate."

"Okay, okay, I can admire your spunk and drive," I said, "but there has to be a ceiling as to how high you can go if you're self-educating."

My father nodded and answered, "I'm not saying that self-educating is solo educating. By self-educating, I'm saying that an individual decides what he or she wants or needs to learn and then goes after it. To some extent, yes, you can do a lot of it on your own. You can read, travel, view films, and listen to educational recordings. Beyond that, you'll need teachers. Certainly I benefited from my instructors at trade school, whom I had to pay out of my own earnings. But plenty of other teachers are always available for free or at very low cost. And a lot of education is free, too."

*Free teachers? Free education?* "Such as?" I asked.

"Reading clubs. Internships. Correspondence courses. Christian education classes. Conferences and conventions. Reserve units in the military. YMCA classes. Public lectures at libraries or art galleries or museums. Plays in the park. Walking tours of city districts. Open air concerts...."

"Whoa!" I interrupted. "Okay, I'll concede that point. Obviously, there is plenty of free education available if you go looking for it. But, playing devil's advocate, isn't the average Joe or Jane prevented from experiencing some high-ticket aspects of education? For example, if I wanted to see Buckingham Palace or the Leaning Tower of Pisa or the pyramids of Egypt, that would take some serious cash. Or let's say I wanted to become a commercial airline pilot. Flight school and hours in the air cost big bucks."

"Yep, those are expensive ventures," my father granted, "but still not impossible to obtain...*for anyone*. It all depends on what you're willing to barter for them."

"Barter?" I echoed. "I didn't know that flight schools and travel agencies were open to barter."

"They aren't. But you can sidestep them with other bartering arrangements. Life is often a series of barters or trade-offs. Even if someone decides to go to a top-notch university, it still becomes a trade-off. That person gives four years of his or her life, and the school provides an education that later is supposed to compensate financially for the time given up in order to complete the degree. I, myself, willingly engaged in life-bartering in order to get some of those 'high ticket' aspects of learning you were talking about."

"You did? In what ways?"

172

"Well, I wanted to visit foreign countries, learn another language, set foot in some major global cities," Dad said. "Of course, I didn't have the money to do that. So, I took advantage of a window of opportunity. In 1944 the federal law stated that anyone who would serve during the War could do so without losing any civilian privileges. I found out that that meant I could enlist in the Navy, and I could still retain my status in the opticians' union without having to pay dues. Additionally, my trade school would have to readmit me upon returning so that I could pick up right where I had left off in my studies—except *then*, I'd be a veteran, and the government would be paying for my education on the GI Bill."

"Wow, some deal," I had to admit. "I mean, so long as you weren't killed or maimed in the war."

"Well, yeah...there *was* that," Dad concurred with a wry smile. "But, praise the Lord, I came out unscathed. I served a little more than a year, and once the war ended, we were all discharged and sent home. However, during that year, I was all over the Atlantic and Pacific oceans. I went through the Panama Canal, stopped in ports in six South American countries, and did some stateside duty in Washington State, California, and Florida. By the time I came home at age eighteen, I'd traveled thousands of miles and had really seen a lot of the world. And it was all free, as a trade-off for my year of military service. I bartered with the government, and we both got a good deal."

## Recognizing Upside Potential

"Did the schooling thing work out when you came home?" I asked.

"Sure did," said Dad. "I stepped right back into night school and earned my certificate, and during the day I was qualified to work as a journeyman optician for much better money than I'd made at the newsstand in the bank. I married your mom in 1946, and two years later you were born, then your brother, then your sister. We bought a nice little house, and I had a steady income. But I wasn't satisfied."

"Really? Why not?" I asked. "Steady paycheck, nice home, a comfortable life.... What was bothering you?"

"Well, it hit me one day that I was in a parallel universe with my former life in the cotton fields."

I wrinkled my forehead. "You've lost me."

"It was like this," he explained. "One day I went to work and sat at the workbench I always sat at. In front of me were blank lenses and a stack of papers containing prescriptions that I needed to grind those lenses to. It was a large room, and there were about forty other opticians working my same shift. At the far end of the room was a door that led to a fancy office. That is where the boss sat each day, going over figures and meeting with clients. He wore an expensive suit, had a mahogany desk and swivel chair, a private phone—which was a big deal in 1953—and a secretary who did his typing and ran his errands.

"I looked around and thought, *Now, there's the guy who's making the real dough around here. The rest of us are day laborers. This is just like picking cotton. If you don't choose to break out, you'll wind up doing the same thing the rest of your life.* It hit me that, just as I had devised a plan to rise above cotton picking, I now had to devise a plan to rise above grinding lenses. During lunch break I asked several other guys if they had any intentions of rising to a manager's position. They looked at me like I was crazy. 'We grind lenses, man. It's dependable employment. Management ain't for our kind.' And it sounded exactly like what I'd heard my friends say when I'd wanted to leave the cotton fields. I realized that I was on my own again, but I also realized that if I had been able to find the upside potential once in life, I could do it again."

I grinned. "Did you also have a cousin who could give you a job in management?"

Dad chuckled. "Nope. But the process was the same as it had been before. It all came down to the fact that *everyone is self-educated.* If I was going to rise in the optical business, I'd have to learn more about it than I currently knew. I decided to take a bold step and go right to the source. I asked for an appointment with the boss, Mr. Meade Ion, owner of the company I worked for. Amazingly, he granted it later that week. I reported to his office at 2:00 p.m. on a Thursday and was shown right in. He shook my hand, said he could give me twenty minutes, and asked point blank what I wanted."

"If you were taking time off *my* work clock, I'd be blunt, too," I interjected, smiling.

"Oh, actually, I liked that about him," my dad said. "I jumped right in. I told him that I admired all that he had built and accomplished, but I didn't want to work for him the rest of my life. I wanted more training, more money, more upside potential. I looked him in the eye and asked, 'If you were just turning twenty-six, as I am, Mr. Ion, and you were in this business, what would you be doing to move up and get ahead?'"

I raised my eyebrows. "Weren't you afraid of offending him by saying you didn't want to work for him all your life?"

"Not really. In fact, that made him laugh," my dad recalled. "He said he was amazed at how many young fellows were willing to do the same redundant work day after day for him. In fact, he joked about how it was odd that a roomful of opticians had no vision for themselves. He then told his secretary to cancel his next appointment, and he spent an hour talking to me. He was full of ideas."

"You're serious?" I said. "He knew you wanted to quit, yet he was helping you?"

My dad nodded. "Yeah, I know it sounds weird, but he said he saw a lot of himself in me, and that other guys had encouraged him, given him advice back when he was my age. It was like he was this fountain of experience waiting for someone to tap into it. He lent me six copies of optometry magazines and circled specific articles I should read about developing technologies. He called a friend who had a lab for specialty problems in optometry and arranged for me to tour the place after work the next day. Then he gave me three books that had nothing to do with the optical profession, but, instead, were on topics like goal setting and leadership and management. He told me not to have tunnel vision, but to see the bigger picture about getting ahead in life."

"Man," I said, "it was like he was becoming your private mentor."

"Exactly," said my dad. "In fact, he met with me five more times to ask about my readings and to answer my questions about business management. Then, he kicked me out."

"He *what*?"

"Well, he told me that I needed more freedom to grow and that my current job of grinding lenses wouldn't provide it. So, he advised me to take a job working for *one* ophthalmologist in a private office as a dispensing optician, even if it meant I had to sell my house and move to another city. This would put me in day-to-day contact with an eye surgeon who could teach me things I wouldn't learn by rubbing elbows with people at my own educational level."

"And you were willing to do that? I think I remember you and Mom telling me back then I'd be changing schools. I remember some sense of anxiety on Mom's part, right?"

"Hey," said my dad, "it wasn't easy selling our house and moving more than one hundred miles away from our friends and neighbors, but when a chance opened up for me to work in a surgeon's office here in Bay City, Michigan, we moved. I spent eight years working with an ophthalmologist, always asking questions, always observing procedures, always taking advantage of self-education. The doctor even sponsored me to attend optical conventions and seminars and conferences. And that's how I learned about the developing field of contact lenses. I felt in my gut that contact lenses would be the dominant product in our industry for the future. I started learning all I could about them. Ironically, many of my colleagues said they were never going to 'take' with the American public. 'People aren't going to place glass directly on their eyes,' they would tell me."

"It does seem strange, when you put it like that," I said. "What made you think otherwise?"

"Because of something I had read in one of the salesmanship books Mr. Ion had lent me," my dad explained. "The author said that when it came to personal vanity, people would pay any amount of money and take any level of risk in order to look better, feel younger, and gain self-confidence. Plastic surgery was proof of that. It was dangerous, costly, and painful, but people all over America paid for it. So, I knew that once a small and safe contact lens could be made—and advertised properly—people would rush to buy it. I wanted to be ready when that high demand began."

## Making Diverse Self-Education Pay Off

"So, how did you get ready" I asked.

"Here's where all the divergent education starting paying off," my dad said. "Keep in mind that I hadn't just been studying aspects of the optical business. I'd also been reading about business, finance, leadership, management, real estate, and customer service. I spent several months putting together a business plan for what would become one of the first contact lens companies in America. I worked out every detail—required office space, necessary equipment, cost of advertising, salaries of employees, licensing agreements, and production schedules. Once I finished it, I hired an accountant to check my figures and a lawyer to read my initial contracts and other legal documents. Both told me that everything was perfect."

"But designing a company on paper..." I began.

"...and actually getting one up and running are two different things," my dad confirmed. "Yeah, only too true. I went hunting for investors. Banks turned me down. Bankers couldn't grasp what a contact lens even was. Private finance companies also turned me down because they insisted I needed some kind of collateral. I had none. After five months of refusals, I sat at my kitchen table one night feeling like a failure. I was so very, very close to becoming a boss, a manager, a true entrepreneur, yet no one could understand my concepts."

"I remember when you started that first business. So, how did you finally get financing?"

Dad smiled. "Your mother made me see the obvious. She said, 'Aren't you talking to the wrong people? I mean, if you want to sell an idea related to the future of the optical business, shouldn't you be talking to people who are already *in* the optical business?' I looked at her, stunned. She was absolutely right. Why hadn't I thought of that? I kissed her and then went off into a back room and stayed up all night revising my sales approach. Three days later, I met with the board of directors of the Phoenix Optical Company and spent two hours pitching my idea. I offered them 80 percent of my company in exchange for start-up costs of $25,000. I then made a two-edged condition. I said that in five years I would double their money, but they would have to allow me to buy them out at that time. I wanted total ownership."

I blinked. "Did they think you were nuts?"

Dad shrugged. "A little cocky, maybe, but not crazy. They knew just enough about the concept of contact lenses to realize it was an area of R & D that warranted exploring. If I already knew how to manufacture and distribute such lenses, it would save them a lot of time. They felt it was worth the gamble. They put up the money. I gave the doctor I was working for sixty days notice, and thereafter I was head honcho of the Phoenix Contact Lens Company."

"Congratulations!" I said, tipping my soda bottle toward him in a tribute salute. Then I paused. "But I seem to remember money was pretty tight when I was in junior high."

"Yeah, the business was far from an instant success," admitted my father. "We lost money the first three years, so I didn't get any raises, much less year-end bonuses. But then, high school girls discovered contact lenses in the early 1960s and they all wanted to get them. They had grown up hearing that guys don't make passes at girls who wear glasses, and whether it was true or not, they wanted contacts. Orders flooded in. I had to hire another helper and we both worked nights and weekends keeping up with the demands on us for production. Two years later, I wrote out a check for $50,000 and bought out my partners and changed the name of the business to the Hensley Contact Lens Company."

"How'd you celebrate?" I asked.

"Two ways," my dad answered, looking aside as though recalling the past. "First, I bought a Lincoln Continental, drove it to Tennessee, and went down that same road above the delta where I used to pick cotton. It wasn't about ego, just the fulfillment of a promise to myself."

I nodded. I would have done the same thing. "And second?"

"I bought a beautiful big mahogany desk and a swivel chair, and I set up a very nice office. I ordered three hand-tailored suits to wear to that office. Oh, and I found the address of Mr. Meade Ion, then retired, and I sent him my business card along with a crate of Florida oranges, a gold pen-and-pencil set, and six silk ties."

## Never Stop Learning

"So, you had arrived, eh?" I surmised.

My dad tilted his head and weighed that a moment.

"Well, yes and no," he said. "I was the owner of a successful company. I had a nice home that was all paid off, and I was even able to purchase a building to move my company into. But the contact lens phenomenon had taught me a lesson. Situations can change on a dime. Just as contact lenses had become the new rage and made traditional eye glasses passé, who was to say that something new would not come in to upstage contact lenses? Besides, I wasn't foolish enough to think I could continue to dominate the market. I estimated, correctly, that it would be only eight or ten years before large pharmaceutical companies would begin to mass produce contact lenses, thus cutting the prices and squeezing out smaller guys like me."

"So, you were hardly started and you already were assuming you were doomed?"

"It's the way of capitalism," said my dad. "Faster, cheaper, more reliable. Someone will always be out to beat you at your own game. Plan for it. Use self-education to move to another level. I did. I continued to run the contact lens business, but I also started to study the field of artificial eyes. Ten years later, when contact lenses had passed their peak for me, I opened an artificial-eye laboratory, and I also started a traditional frame-and-lenses business again. Whatever your needs, whatever your age, I could serve you."

I scanned Dad's office with a better comprehension of what I was looking at. His framed awards had new context for me. The mahogany desk was suddenly symbolic. Even the business cards with his name as CEO there on his desk seemed to have greater authority. I shook my head in amazement and respect. "You were always adapting, always applying what you'd learned to developing circumstances, is that it?"

"Always," confirmed my dad. "I began to experiment with ways to photograph healthy eyes so as to create an artificial eye that was a better match. I worked with Lucite instead of glass for lighter weight, better shaping, and stronger texture. I formulated a way to mix tiny red threads into the white Lucite to give the artificial eye a more realistic composition. I published my findings in leading optical journals, and I was asked to speak at seminars at national optical conventions and deliver lectures at Ferris State University as an adjunct professor."

"All with no formal education," I summarized.

"*Au contraire*," argued my father. "I had plenty of formal education. I just didn't have any college degrees. Don't confuse the two. And never forget that in the final analysis, *everyone is self-educated.*"

So, we did it his way. During college years I lived at home, taught guitar lessons part time at a local music store, bought myself a Mustang, and earned an associate of arts degree from Delta Community College. In the summers I worked as a salesman for my dad's companies, and he taught me the ins and outs of running a business. Meanwhile, several of my friends who had gone to large universities either washed out for poor grades or ran out of cash and came home. I'd see them working at department stores, restaurants, and lawn care services around town. Another guy became a cop, one girl became the assistant manager of a print shop, and several others started working on the line at the General Motors factory in our city.

With my dad's continual encouragement, I transferred to a local four year college, paid off my car by still working part time, went to summer school to be ahead of schedule, and finished a bachelor's degree three and a half years after graduating from high school. I had two college diplomas and no debt. My father, as could be imagined, was proud of me for all I'd achieved.

My high school friends who did finish at the large universities came home and, indeed, they had degrees in elementary education or accounting or pre-law or pre-med. But they also had thousands of dollars of debt. I would meet them from time to time, and it always made me appreciate my dad all the more when I discovered that none of them had become another Albert Einstein or Marie Curie or Pablo Picasso or Margaret Mitchell by attending the big name schools. In fact, I was hard pressed to see any way they were any farther ahead in life than I was.

I also followed Dad's footsteps by entering the military—although I served a couple of years in the Army instead of the Navy, and my overseas experience was a year of duty in Vietnam. In that process I was able to visit fourteen different countries while on leave or R & R or when transferring to new duty stations. When I came home and got married, the GI Bill allowed me to complete a master's degree in English from Central Michigan University in eleven months. Later, amidst the arrival of two kids and working for a newspaper and, after that, serving as a public relations director at a small college, I finished a doctoral degree in literature and linguistics from Ball State University. Each time, thanks to what Dad taught me, I came out of school debt free.

My father also passed on to me his constant passion to go to the next level. I never drove my car without listening to a book on tape. Everyone I worked for wound up being my mentor, because I always asked a lot of questions. I read books outside of my field. I traveled more. College provided the basic structure for course work, but, always, my *education* came from my personal in-depth studies.

I've never attended a Big Ten or Ivy League college, but heeding my father's advice concerning self-education has enabled me to write more than fifty books, and be a guest professor or writer in residence at more than sixty colleges, including Oxford University. I never would have dreamed it back when I was enrolling in community college, but currently I'm a full professor at Taylor University and director of its professional writing department.

In 1990, a Big Ten school, Indiana University, bestowed upon me its "Award for Teaching Excellence." At the banquet in my honor, I was asked, "What has been the secret of your success, Dr. Hensley?" I thought of my father, and without hesitation I responded, "I had the advantage of being self-educated."

## Key Points Found in Section *8*

1. In the final analysis, every person is self-educated.

2. You don't have to go to school to become *educated*.

3. Teachers are always available, and books are always free.

4. If you don't gain an education in America, it's your own fault.

5. It comes down to what you know, what you can do, and how well you can do it.

6. Life is often a series of barters or trade-offs.

7. Always look for something that has upside potential.

8. People will pay any amount of money and taken any kinds of risks in order to look younger, feel better, and gain self-confidence.

9. Be open to all learning, at all times, in all places, from all people.

10. Divergent education is not hodgepodge education. It's a cornucopia of learning.

11. It's not about ego. It's about fulfilling promises to yourself.

12. Situations can change on a dime, so never stop learning.

*Elroy Bellam was already weaving by the time he entered the doorway of the Skull Boys' gang headquarters in the area of the inner city that once had been known as The Projects. He had finished off a third of a bottle of Jack Daniels, and had it not been for his faithful German shepherd, Sugar, who knew the route and kept him pointed in the right direction, Elroy might never have made it.*

*Zipper Moby, the gang's leader, waved Elroy forward. "Shoot, boy, you a bigger idiot than I thought. You still set on goin' through with this?"*

*"Not a moments...hesitation," responded Elroy. "Already dressed for the occasion." He opened his dark raincoat. Twenty-six interlaced sticks of dynamite covered his torso.*

*"Whoa, fool! Why you comin' in here like that!" Behind him, enveloped in a cloud of cigarette smoke, four other gang members looked up from their card game. To the side of them, sporting do-rags and wifebeaters, two other gang members were battling each other at a video game while hip-hop blared in the background.*

*"Not hooked up yet," said Elroy with a stupid grin. He fumbled in his pocket and eventually managed to extricate a switch box with extended wires. "Need you...help me get connected."*

"Not inside here, I ain't. How'd you come up with this stupid plan anyway?"

Elroy tapped the side of his head with his index finger. "Watchin' TV, brother. It's all there. They do this stuff all time over in them places like Africanistan and Iraniwaki. Some guy puts on a vest of dynamite, walks into a pizza parlor, and ... and ka-boom...everybody toast."

Zipper squinted. "That right, fool, includin' the dude wearing the vest."

Elroy shook his head slowly. "Don't make no difference, Blood. Them white boys killed my little brother Marcus, so they gotta pay. They moved into a storefront over on Jordan Avenue. Man, that's cross the street from our territory. Can't allow that. No, no, can't allow that. They gotta go."

"So, what you gonna do? Walk in there—a black dude in shades and a raincoat—and say, 'Good mornin', Gents,' and then set yourself off like a Roman candle? You think that how it gonna go down?"

"Better plan than that." Elroy groped and found his bottle, removed the cap and took a long swig.

He wiped his mouth, but kept the bottle in his hand. "All's I gotta do is get down on that street. If'n I get within fifty feet of that place, it all goin' down. Boom, boom, boom. What the blast don't kill, the fallin' building will. Got it all worked out. Oh, yeah, all worked out." Again he tapped his temple before taking another swig.

*"Okay, okay," said Zipper, "these skinheads with the dragon tattoos, they done your little brother Marcus. But ain't it a bit of overkill to take out couple dozen of them in return?"*

*Elroy's eyes narrowed in anger. "Sends a message! Pushes 'em back to their own side of town. They ain't welcome here."*

*"But they ain't crossed that street yet, Elroy. They still outside our territory. When Marcus was robbin' that grocery store, he was on <u>their</u> turf. Bad luck that one of them Spiders was patrollin' just when Marcus was waving his gun in the face of that old lady. Marcus shot first. The dude dropped him. End of episode. Switch channels."*

*"He...only fourteen," said Elroy, tears forming in his eyes. "Somebody got to pay for that. Ain't right. Today... payback time." He took another swallow from the whiskey bottle. "You gonna help me or not?"*

*Zipper looked over his shoulder. The four other gang members sat huddled around the card table still playing poker. No one said anything. One shrugged, another nodded. No words, though.*

*Zipper let out a long sigh. "You know we gonna take care of your mama, right?"*

*Elroy nodded. "And I got a cousin, Marcel. He livin' over on...."*

*"I know where your cousin livin,'" said Zipper. "Okay, we keep an eye on him, too."*

"Come on, Sugar, we got a schedule to keep." Elroy nudged the dog and she moved outside, careful to keep her body in contact with Elroy, lest he veer off somewhere. Zipper followed, holding the arming device. After they had gone four blocks, they came to an alley that was always dark, day or night.

"Here's your path, Elroy. You leavin' the dog behind?"

"I'll send her back once I get there," Elroy said. "I...I know I gettin' drunk, so she'll keep me on the straight and narrow. Come over here and let me show you how to put on those wires."

"How'd a maintenance guy like you get this much dynamite, anyway?" asked Zipper.

"Sold all I owned," Elroy answered flatly. "Won't be needin' nothin' from now on. And, if you got the money, you can buy anything. Met a dude, just when I needed him most." He motioned one hand. "Here, wait. 'Fore you connect that second wire, put a piece of this electrical tape against the switch. Don't want it accidentally goin' off 'fore I get to the blast zone."

"Suits me," said Zipper. He made some moves. "Okay, man, you wired now. But you change your mind, just come on back. Ain't nobody gonna say you a coward."

"Ain't comin' back. Nothin' to bury either. Elroy Bellam, the human cannonball. Goin' all the way."

"Well," said Zipper, "I'd wish you luck, but ain't no point in that, is there, heh?"

*Elroy put the wired trigger mechanism inside his pocket, took another long pull on the bottle, then flashed a thumbs-up. "Don't need no luck at this point. Them white boys over on Jordan Avenue…they's the ones gonna need some luck today." He nudged the dog. "Lead on, Sugar."*

*Dutifully, Sugar entered the alley. It was dark, but the dog's keen eyes and acute sense of smell made it easy for her to follow a route she and Elroy had traversed on several occasions. By now, Elroy was feeling lightheaded and starting to swerve. Occasionally he paused to maintain his balance. Each time he stopped, however, he took a swig from his now half-empty bottle.*

*They made it down the first long alley, and then back out into the bright sunlight. Elroy groped for Sugar's coat, letting her lead him across the street like a leader dog with a blind man. Even though Elroy was only twenty-four, he'd had the dog for twelve years, given to him by a protective uncle who felt a canine bodyguard would be appropriate for young Elroy in the neighborhood he would be growing up in. As it turned out, Sugar never attacked anyone and had proven more valuable as a four-footed GPS in getting Elroy back home after many a night of heavy drinking with friends.*

*They entered the second alley, and Elroy stumbled forward.*

*"I am gonna rain down my curses on 'em today, Sugar. They ain't gonna know what hit 'em. Yes, sirree, it goin' to be a sight to be-hold." He chuckled in a drunken haze, imagining*

*flying bodies and crumbling buildings, bursting windows, and upended automobiles.*

*Suddenly, sensing danger, Sugar froze. Like a bird dog, she went into a pointer's position, peering into the darkness of the alley. There, blocking the passageway, stood the shimmering form of a man holding a gleaming, razor-sharp stiletto. The man looked directly at Sugar and shook his head. Obediently, Sugar halted. This was no street ragamuffin she could bark at and scare away. Neither was this a cop. They all smelled like aftershave, doughnuts, and gun oil. It wasn't a rival gang member either. They were noisy, did a lot of swaggering, and gave off strong body odor.*

*No, this was a man the likes of whom Sugar had never encountered, and, instinctively, she knew he was to be obeyed. This was the end of the line today for her and for Elroy.*

*Sugar moved in front of Elroy, preventing him from stepping ahead.*

*"What you doin', Sugar?" demanded Elroy. "Get out of my way. Move it, you crazy mutt."*

*The dog was unswayed. She continued to block Elroy's path.*

*"I said for you to move, Dog!" Elroy was worried he might lose his resolve if he stopped. There could be no delay. He had to maintain forward momentum.*

*Adamantly, Sugar stood sure-footed in front of Elroy. Frustrated, Elroy first cuffed the dog in the head, and when that didn't work, he kicked Sugar in the side. The dog winced in pain and yielded the path. Elroy grabbed her by the coat and flung her. "Get out there."*

*Sugar now hobbled forward and brought Elroy to the end of the second alley, and, once again, letting him grab her coat, led him across the bright street and into a third alley. Elroy was babbling, half talking and half singing, making no sense, yet still taking regular drinks from the bottle, which was nearly empty.*

*Halfway down this new alley, the illuminated figure appeared once more. He communicated to Sugar's mind: "I am Jesus. What your master is doing is wrong. Do not go forward. Stop him now."*

*The hair on Sugar's back rose and her eyes narrowed. Without hesitation, she turned and shoved her entire body mass against Elroy. He crashed into the side of the brick building that bordered the alleyway. The dog did her best to keep him pinned.*

*"What is wrong with you!" demanded Elroy. "You actin' crazy!" Seeing a broken broom handle on the ground, he grabbed it up and hit Sugar on the head and back and rump. "Get off me! Get off! You gone blind or somethin'? Back off." He struck the dog so hard, she had no choice but to retreat from the blows. For good measure, Elroy, now both confused and angry, kicked the dog. Sugar whined and limped forward. "We gots two more blocks to go, then you can go back, you yellow-*

bellied, mangy mutt. Why you turnin' against me after all the years we been together? Fool dog."

Once again Sugar led Elroy through the dark alley, across a bright street, and into the next dark alley. Scared, baffled, and unnerved, the dog was on full alert. Disobeying the stranger was unthinkable, but each time she'd done her best to protect her master, Elroy had beaten her. What to do, what to do? Cautiously, she crept forward, Elroy now weaving worse than ever.

Suddenly, the glowing man materialized once again, standing astride the path, blocking the way down the alley. Sugar trembled in fear. She knew she could not move forward, but she was too loyal to abandon Elroy. She merely stopped in her tracks.

"What! Again?" Elroy raised the piece of broom handle and brought it down on Sugar's back. It knocked the breath out of her, and she dropped, unable to rise. "Get up! Get up, you stupid dog or I'll beat you to death."

Slowly, Sugar turned her head upward and said, "Why do you keep hitting me, Elroy?"

"Why?" he screamed back. "Because you won't obey me. You keep causin' me trouble."

"But haven't I always been good to you, loyal to you? Why would you think I'd turn against you on our last day together?"

"I don't know," said Elroy, "but you have. And furthermore...."

*Elroy stopped in mid-sentence. He squinted at Sugar. His eyes crossed then uncrossed. He shook his head and then leaned forward and looked closer at the dog. He straightened and looked at the almost empty bottle of whiskey in his hand. As if it had suddenly turned into a burning lump of coal, he flung it away. It shattered against the brick wall.*

*"Ayyyy…ayyyy," he babbled. "What's goin' on here!" In a panic, he raised the stick over Sugar again. "You not gonna get me, demon dog."*

*"Stop!" The commanding, reverberating voice halted Elroy in mid-swing. "You strike that dog one more time, and you'll feel the business end of this blade."*

*Elroy peered into the darkness. He could see some kind of form in the shape of a man. Sort of illuminated, with a kind of a glow that made him visible, even in the darkened alleyway. Slowly, ever so slowly, Elroy lowered the broomstick and let it clatter to the pavement.*

*"That dog is the only reason you're not dead already," said the stranger. "She's the best friend you've ever had. She has acted far more nobly than you have, so don't press your luck."*

*Elroy knew he was drunk. Yeah, sure. But drunk or not, he could never remember hallucinating before. What came next, dancing pink elephants or maybe little green men in flying ships? He shook his head and whapped himself upside the noggin a couple of times to try to clear the cobwebs. "Who are you?" he asked. He blinked several times.*

*The figure moved closer. "Think of me as the Negotiator. The Prince of Peace."*

*Elroy weighed that a moment. "You in a band?"*

*"No," said Jesus. "Just a host." He gave a low whistle, and Sugar rose and came to him. He put his hands on the dog and rubbed her vigorously. The dog responded immediately, gaining strength. She licked the face of Jesus, and Jesus smiled. He pointed down the opposite end of the alley. "Go home now." The dog took a quick look at Elroy and another glance back at Jesus before trotting away along the route she had just come. In seconds, she was gone.*

*Jesus folded the switchblade stiletto and stuffed it in his boot. "Come on, Elroy. I'm going to walk with you for awhile."*

*"You with them white boys?" asked Elroy. "Your hair ain't like them, and you ain't got all them crazy tattoos. Still, you could be workin' with them white boys."*

*"Red, brown, yellow, black, and white," replied Jesus, "they are precious in my sight. I play no favorites. Come on. Walking will help you sober up a bit."*

*"So...so, where we goin'?"*

*"Same place you've been heading. To visit those skinheads, the Spiders."*

*Elroy whirled. "Say what! How...how you know about that?"*

*"Déjà vu,"* Jesus whispered to himself. *"I was going through this identical scene just twenty-four hours ago with a member of the Spiders, right here. A Saint Bernard that time, though."*

*"I said, how you be knowin' about where I'm headin' now?" repeated Elroy.*

*"Look closely," said Jesus. "Remember me?" He gave Elroy a minute. "I'm the guy who sold you the dynamite."*

*Elroy glared at the man and then blanched. "Hey! You him! You took my money."*

*"Here, you can have it back," said Jesus. "You're going to need it. You're not going to die today."*

*He stuffed a wad of bills in Elroy's pocket and at the same time took out the detonator and pulled off the protective tape.*

*"Go easy with that," cautioned Elroy. He licked his lips and felt sweat on his forehead.*

*"What? This?" Jesus grinned, very unconcerned, and then flipped the switch.*

*In his terror, Elroy almost fainted, wetting his pants as he fell against the brick wall.*

*"Whoa, hey, get hold of yourself," said Jesus. "You didn't think I'd sell you genuine explosives, did you?"*

*Elroy tried to speak, but no words would form. His stomach sent acid into his mouth. It wasn't the booze. It was the terror of this man. Prince of Peace, my foot! Man, this guy was the voice of doom.*

"Come on," said Jesus, kindly. "Let's get you out of this tangled mess." He drew Elroy forward, pulled off the raincoat, and untangled layers of Velcro, string, and tape that held the sticks of fake dynamite in place. "See, isn't that much more comfortable?" Jesus walked to a dumpster and threw the harmless cylinders inside. Folding the coat, he walked back to Elroy and handed it to him. "Just throw this over your arm. You won't be needing it today. It's nice out. Come on, let's get going."

"You…you took my power," Elroy protested feebly. "Ain't got no reason to go nowhere now."

"Sure, you do," said Jesus. "Remember what you told your dog? You're going to rain down curses on the Spiders."

"I hate those guys. They kill my little brother."

"Yes, I know. Marcus shouldn't have been robbing that store, and he shouldn't have fired his gun at Rodney."

"Rodney? Who he?"

"Flint Face is his street name," said Jesus. "He's an undercover cop. He infiltrates gangs and keeps the authorities informed about potential problems. Marcus wasn't killed by an actual gang member."

"Make no difference. He white, so he my enemy."

"Well, it looks like nothing I say will change your mind, so I guess I'll just leave you for now."

*Elroy looked puzzled. "What? You just walkin' off now?"*

*"Later, Elroy," said Jesus, as he walked into the shadows and seemed to evaporate.*

*Suddenly, Elroy had the worst hangover he'd ever known. He leaned forward and vomited, then staggered forward and fell, gashing his head deeply on the sharp corner of the dumpster. Blood oozed down his face. He was too weak to stand, too sick at his stomach to move. He could barely whisper a cry of help.*

*He lay suffering for at least twenty minutes, when, to his amazement, Zipper arrived on the scene.*

*"Oh, brother, you a sight for sore eyes," said Elroy, moaning. "Get me out of here. I need a hospital."*

*Zipper looked up and down the alleyway. "Your dog come back without you. We didn't hear no explosion. What'd you do, you drunken fool? We thought you got caught by the law, maybe was gonna rat us out. That what happened, Elroy? You sell out to the law?"*

*Elroy coughed. "What you talkin' about, man? You know I ain't no snitch." He coughed again, deeper, more congested. "I'm sick, and you gotta get me to a doctor."*

*"I ain't gotta do nothin' for a loser like you," said Zipper. "Only maybe I should finish you right now." He pulled a nickle-plated revolver from his waistband. "Two rounds to*

*the back of your head and we ain't got no more worries about a stoolie."*

*"You talkin' crazy," said Elroy, wheezing. "First, you tryin' to talk me out of killin' myself. Now you here saying you gonna whack me yo'self. I need a doctor."*

*Zipper looked at the pathetic figure and smirked. "You ain't even worth a bullet. The way you bleedin', you gonna be dead soon anyway. Let the rats finish you. S'long, Elroy...the human cannonball what blowed hisself up. Ha!"*

*Zipper looked up and down the alleyway, then hightailed it back the way he had come. Elroy watched him disappear into the distance. Blood continued to ooze from his head wound. He slipped in and out of consciousness.*

*A sharp kick to his legs brought Elroy conscious again.*

*"What do we got here? Wake-up, wino," came the voice of a stranger. Elroy tried to focus. After several seconds, he realized he was looking up at two private security guards, one white, one African-American.*

*"I need help," Elroy said, trying to extend a hand.*

*"You smell like a saloon," said the African-American guard. "Why don't you stay down there and sleep it off?"*

*Elroy was panic stricken. "No...no," he rasped, "don't leave me. Gotta get to a doctor."*

*"Oh, sure," mocked the Anglo guard. "Just give us a minute, and we'll go get our car and take you to the emergency room."*

*Elroy tried to think. "Hey," he said, softly. "I can pay you. I got money. Really."*

*"No, you don't," said the mocking guard. "We already rolled you and found the cash in your coat pocket. Nearly four hundred bucks. Obviously, you're either a dealer or a pimp. You made somebody very unhappy and you got your head kicked in. Not our problem, amigo. Next time—if there is one—choose your enemies more carefully."*

*"We have to come back through here again in an hour," said the other guard. "If you're not gone, we're going to throw you into that dumpster where trash like you belongs. The city can dispose of you on Monday."*

*The twosome started to walk away. Elroy tried to call after them, but he had no strength, no voice.*

*He was woozy, feverish, exhausted. Again, he passed out.*

*Seconds, minutes, days, and years drifted forward and backward, moving in slow motion, and Elroy dreamed of his younger days, when he'd lived in The Projects with kids of all ethnic backgrounds—Poles, Germans, Jews, Italians, African-Americans, and even a couple of red-headed Irish kids. They'd played stickball and relays and marbles and tag, and they'd gone to each other's houses for meals, and there were no color problems, no bigotry. Just kids playing and laughing. Then came the recessions, the layoffs, the bad times, and then the forming of all the gangs, and it got all jumbled and mixed up, and everybody got separated and isolated, and friends became enemies, and neighborhoods became war zones, and he'd lost his best friends and his little brother had been killed, and....*

*Interrupting Elroy's delirium was the sensation of someone helping him lift his head and take sips of delicious cold water.*

*"Easy does it, lad," said the soothing male voice. "Ya got yerself a nasty gash there, you do. Here we go then, eh, one more little taste. There's me boyo. Good man, yourself, Elroy."*

*At the sound of his name, Elroy tried to focus on his rescuer. Dried blood seemed to have glued together one set of eyelids, but with his other eye he could make out the dreaded visage of one of the skinheads. He wanted to resist, to defend himself, but he had no strength. Besides, the man wasn't attacking him, he was actually giving him a drink of water.*

*"Here, let's get your face cleaned up a bit," said the skinhead. He poured water onto a handkerchief and began to wipe the grime and dried blood from Elroy's face.*

*"You...uh...how you know my name?"*

*The skinhead smiled. "Your name? Why, Elroy, m'friend, do ya not know me? We're both a tad older, we are, but we're still chums, tell me so. It's Mikey, your old neighbor. Mike Murphy. You used to play kick-the-can with me and me brothers."*

*Elroy was now able to open both eyes slightly. He focused. "Mikey? No...can't be. It's you, man? This ain't no dream?"*

*"From the looks of you, dear boyo, it's more like a nightmare. How'd ya get yerself in such a mess, be tellin' me now."*

*"Robbed…beaten…left for dead,"* Elroy *mumbled, trying to put the past day back together.*

*"Well, I'll be takin' care of ya now, laddie," said Mike. "Can ya stand? Can ya walk?"*

*Elroy made an effort to rise, but pain pounded his head like a sledge hammer, knocking him to the ground. He was aware of nothing more until he awoke several hours later.*

*First one eye opened, then the other. He was in a small room, sparse but clean. He could smell coffee. Slowly, he lifted his hand and touched his head. Gauze wrappings covered his forehead and skull.*

*"Awake at last, are we?" asked Mike Murphy, coming over to sit on the side of the bed. "No, don't move too quickly. Let me help you. There's a good lad." He propped the pillows and gently helped Elroy into a sitting position. "Here ya go. Fresh brewed. Take it black, do ya?"*

*Elroy accepted the proffered mug in two hands and swallowed once, then again. It tasted like nectar.*

*"Where…how long I been…?"*

*"You're in Mike's room with the skinheads at the Spiders' headquarters," came a voice behind Mike. Elroy moved his head slightly and was amazed to see the dynamite guy— that glowing guy from the alley—seated in the corner. "He's*

been nursing you for the past several hours. You would have died if he hadn't come along, brought you back here, and given you some medical help."

Elroy was too confused to say anything.

"Me friend here," said Mike, nodding slightly toward Jesus, "told me where to find ya. Told me to take a bottle of water and some bandages. Had to cross Jordan Avenue to locate ya, which these days is No Man's Land. But, hey, we were boyo neighbors once, and that counts fer somethin', am I right abou' that?"

"The others," whispered Elroy. "My friend Zipper… the security cops…they left me to die. You the one what saved me, Mikey?"

Jesus rose and approached the bed. "So, who's your friend, Elroy? Who do you want around here as your neighbor? Let me hear you rain down your curses."

Elroy looked at Mike, sitting there shaved bald, his arms covered with tattoos of dragons, swords, lightning bolts, and skulls. "You a good man, Mikey," was all Elroy could say.

"That didn't come out as a curse," said Jesus. "Try again."

Elroy ignored the gibe and kept looking into the eyes of his long-lost buddy, his childhood companion. He said, "It good to see you again, Mikey. I 'member the days, bro'. Yeah, I 'member the days. Good days, they was."

206

*"Nope, that was definitely not a curse, Elroy," insisted Jesus. "Can you try once more, this time with a little more venom?"*

*Feeling stronger, Elroy sat upright. He reached out his hand, and Mike took it. They didn't shake. They just held onto one another, bonding, bridging, reaffirming all that had been good about their youth. "I love ya, man," said Elroy. "You saved my life. Yeah...yeah, welcome back to the neighborhood."*

*"Peace, m'man," said Mike. He leaned over and gave Elroy a tight hug and a slap on the back.*

*Elroy smiled. "Man, I'm hungry. You gotta cafe near here?"*

*"Two doors down," said Mike. "Got yer sea legs, yet?"*

*Elroy leaned against Mike at first, but then gained his equilibrium. Jesus held the door open as the two friends walked out. Once they all had gained the sidewalk, Jesus said, "I'll leave you two to catch up on news. I've got a business I need to get back to." He turned and started heading up the street.*

*"Hey, 'fore you go, one more thing," called Elroy. "Back when we was in the alley, I know I was pretty wasted, but did that dog...uh...well, did that dog actually...uh...?"*

*Without turning around, Jesus said, "Lay off the booze, Elroy. It can do strange things to your head."*

207

## SECTION 9

## SUCCESSFUL NEGOTIATING: *YET* IS A SELF-EMPOWERING WORD

I once knew a man who was not afraid to say, "I don't know." This rather amazed me at the time because most folks—men in particular—usually don't like to admit they are not up to speed or fully knowledgeable about something. This is especially true if they are questioned by a boss or client.

When I first met the man, I was fresh out of college, recently married, and working as an assistant office manager at an electric company. Although this was a temporary position for me while I waited to begin my doctoral studies, it proved to be a great learning experience. My direct supervisor, a man in his forties named Larry, was the liaison between our electric company and all clients—both current and potential clients.

One afternoon we were in an important meeting. A potential client wanted to know if our company was big enough and competent enough to install all of the power lines needed for a new shopping mall. If we landed this job, it would mean about three years of high-paying steady employment. But we were just one of six other electric companies trying to win the contract.

The spokesman for the client presented us with a very tricky request. It related to electrical wiring that would have to be placed inside of a water tower. If not done perfectly, the job could prove to be dangerous, even fatal.

"So, here's what I want to know," said the client. "Can your people install this wiring according to these specifications and do it within the cost parameters we need to hold to?" He looked directly at Larry, my supervisor.

Larry examined the blueprints more closely, took out a calculator and punched in some numbers, then looked up eye to eye with the client. Speaking with confidence and honesty he replied, "I don't know—*yet.*" He paused and then added, "I can get you an answer. It will be a definitive one that my company will stand by. I don't know what that answer will be just yet, but within twenty-four hours, I can get back to you. I'll make this my top priority for the next day."

The client looked at Larry for a moment, weighed his response, then nodded. "Fair enough. Call me back at this time tomorrow and let me know your answer." They shook hands and we left.

For the next two continuous shifts, Larry and our team made phone calls to suppliers, ran numbers with our staff accountants, had meetings with our engineers, and showed the plans to our construction and maintenance supervisors. Larry got his bottom-line plans about how we would do the job and what we would need to charge. He called the client, who thanked us for our feedback and bid. Ten days later, we received a call that the job was ours.

## The *Yet* Factor

Since learning this negotiating technique from Larry many years ago, I have employed the word *yet* on many occasions. Adding *yet* to responses offers honesty about a current situation while simultaneously implying optimism and confidence about being able to resolve an issue or provide a service.

Saying *yet* buys time. The trick is, you need to be able to convince your listener that momentum, forward drive, and a plan of action already in the works will warrant granting you some extra leeway. Note that when Larry had to respond to the potential client's question, he took a few moments to examine the blueprints and to do some initial estimates before saying, "I don't know—*yet.*" This wasn't merely staging or stalling; rather, it was genuine analysis of a specific opportunity. It gave the impression that he had enough basic understanding of the problem so that, if given more time, he could come up with an accurate assessment and response. That's all people need: a belief that you have grasped the initial dilemma and you are up to the task of responding.

Sometimes this strategy can help you meet an emotional challenge. If you ask for your girlfriend's hand in marriage and her dad asks, "Can you afford to take care of a wife?" your honest response may be, "No—not *yet*." Then you can add, "But if we get married next summer, I'll be out of college and so will she. We'll both have jobs, and we'll do just fine."

Sometimes it can relate to a business challenge. A convention manager may approach you and ask, "Is your florist service big enough to handle decorations for this summer's Miss Teen America competition?" Your answer would be, "No—not *yet*." Then you can add, "But if you can secure a contract for us for next summer, we can lock in a price and I'll be able to hire the needed personnel and have a year to plan a wide variety of displays for you."

Sometimes it can relate to a health challenge. Your employer may ask, "Do you feel ready to come back to work?" Your answer might be, "Honestly, no—not *yet*" Then you can add, "I'm glad you are still holding a place for me, and I will be eager to do as good a job as I did before the car accident. But my physician says I'll need another three months of physical therapy. I'm going to stay faithful to the regimen, and once she pronounces me 'fit' again, I'll call you about a return date for my work."

It takes some guts to say you don't have an answer or you aren't ready to take action, but it relieves you of a lot of tension if you are honest with people about the reality of a situation. Most people are willing to grant you time to do a job correctly if you explain your intention to have integrity in responding to their questions about time, costs, personnel, plans, and materials.

## Using *Yet* for Self-Improvement

A corollary to this principle is that you also can inspire and motivate yourself by using the word *yet*. If you haven't received a promotion at your job, encourage yourself by saying, "I haven't *yet* worked here as long as most of the other employees. However, I'm establishing a good track record, so my promotion is bound to come soon." Or, if you are working at losing weight, say, "I haven't lost twenty-five pounds *yet*, but I've been dropping a pound a week with my new walking program, so if I stay at it, I'll hit my goal in just a couple of more months."

Likewise, we can use *yet* as a harbinger of potential success. When Revolutionary War leader John Paul Jones was asked if he was ready to surrender, his reply was, "I have not *yet* begun to fight." We can take the same approach to challenges. Tell yourself, "Sure, I work hard and achieve a lot, but I am completing my master's degree in business, and my best years are *yet* to come." The word *yet* provides a future vision of excellent advancement.

There is no shame in candidly admitting that you are not ready to give an answer to a question or provide a solution to a problem, so long as you imply that you are capable of coming back later with an intelligent response. The word *yet* buys you that time. Use it as *yet* another dependable communication option.

## Key Points Found in Section 9

1. *Yet* is a self-empowering word.

2. Adding *yet* to responses offers honesty while implying optimism and confidence.

3. Saying *yet* buys you time.

4. The trick is to convince your listener there is momentum, drive, and an action plan already in the works.

5. People need a belief that you have grasped the dilemma and you are up to responding.

6. Using *yet* relieves a lot of tension if you are honest with people about a situation.

7. You can inspire and motivate yourself by using the word *yet*.

8. You can use *yet* as a harbinger of potential success.

*A large crowd had gathered for the groundbreaking of what would be the new wing of Tree of Life Furnishings. Pete Fishers and Jesus were watching as a dump truck unloaded a fifth delivery of crushed stones.*

*"You're really into these gravel foundations, aren't you?" mused Pete.*

*Jesus nodded and said, "A wise man builds his...."*

*"Yeah, yeah," interrupted Pete with a dismissive wave of his hand. "So you've told us a hundred times." He glanced down at his electronic tablet. "Okay, look, we gotta stay on schedule. You know what a nutcase Feingold is about routines and systems. He's got the whole day planned out."*

*"There is a time for every purpose under heaven," said Jesus.*

*"May be," said Pete. "If so, Feingold's got it on this grid. I never seen such a fanatic for detail." He paused, looked around, then leaned close. In a conspiratorial whisper he said, "He's writin' a book about you. Seriously. Other day, I was in his office during lunch hour, and I seen his computer screen when he was out for coffee. Know what he was writin' about you?"*

*"My genealogy?" speculated Jesus.*

*"Naw, naw, I don't think he knows nothin' about that DNA stuff and all that cloning they talk about on TV. Uh-uh,*

*no. He was lookin' up your family tree. You know, like your grandparents and great-grandparents and stuff like that."*

*"I'm sure you were bored."*

*"Yep. Don't make no difference to me who your old man was. Who cares, right? I mean, what's important is what we're doin' right now, building the company, givin' people jobs, producin' products we can take pride in." He hesitated, then added, "I mean, I met your folks a time or two. Nice people, don't get me wrong. Although that mom of yours can be a little bossy. Still, my point is, if I was writin' a book about you—and who knows, I just might someday—I wouldn't fill it up with a list of relatives. Nope, I'd get to the point."*

*"You usually do," said Jesus.*

*"Say again?"*

*"I've seen the memos and letters you've written to some of the employees, both stateside and overseas. You do a good job of expressing what we're all about as a company, what our mission is. I'm sure Martha has to clean up the grammar before she sends them out, but your message is solid." He waited a beat then asked, "Can I make a suggestion?"*

*"I'm listenin'."*

*"Save all those letters. Not just as computer files. Make separate copies for yourself. Some people aren't book writers, but their letters can be just as valuable. You're more the letter-writing type."*

*"Think so, eh? Hmm. Yeah, I'll do that. Just might need 'em someday."*

*"Just might," Jesus agreed.*

*"By the way," asked Pete, "what does* <u>begat</u> *mean?"*

*Suddenly, they heard a command issued by someone with a bullhorn. "All executive board members, please come to the paving area of the new wing. Please come to the paving area of the new wing."*

*"That's you," said Jesus.*

*"Don't seem right," argued Pete, moving out. "How come, if you founded the company, came up with all the product ideas, and got everything rollin', you don't wanna put your name in the wet concrete with the rest of us? Seems like it should be your name and yours alone."*

*Jesus walked beside Pete. "I told you right from the start, I'll be with you a short while, and then I'll leave everything for you and the other men to handle. You fellows will carry on the work when I'm gone."*

*Pete furrowed his brow and put a hand on Jesus' shoulder. "But, I don't want you leavin' us. You ain't just a boss, you're more like a teacher."*

*"You call me teacher. That pleases me. And it's accurate. But, in time, the student must become the teacher. And your time is coming."*

*"Does it* <u>have</u> *to be like that?" said Pete. "Set in stone?"*

*Jesus nodded to where fresh concrete was being poured. "It soon will be."*

*When they arrived at what was to be the entrance for the new wing, the others were already gathered round in* the brilliant, hot sunlight. John Brothers, Matt Feingold, and Sy Zylotski were in Hawaiian shirts and holding bottles of ice water. Andy Fishers, sporting designer sunglasses and a Panama hat, nursed a tall glass of lemonade. The other execs were in casual summer dress, including baseball hats, shorts, sandals, and tee-shirts. Only Judas wore lightweight slacks, a linen shirt, and serge sport coat. Under duress, he had given up the tie this once.

Forming a ring at the group's edge were more than two hundred fifty employees there to observe the big event. Work had been called off for the rest of the afternoon.

"Okay," announced Pete, "accordin' to the agenda, the twelve of us need to pick up one of these shovels, scoop out some dirt, and pose for the cameras." Jonathan and Barney emerged from the crowd, one with a camera and the other with a camcorder. They signaled they were ready.

The execs retrieved the shovels and aligned themselves, their feet ready to push the blades into the earth. Many of the bystanders were already recording the event with their personal cameras and phones. "Sure you won't join us, Boss?" called Nate.

"I'll stay here in the shade," said Jesus. "I'd rather not draw attention to myself. Dig in."

After several serious poses, the execs began to ham it up for the cameras. They had so much fun lifting bottled drinks in mock salutes and crossing shovel handles in sham swordfights, *they didn't even notice Jesus had disappeared. It wasn't until a stranger approached Pete and Matt and pointedly asked to talk to Jesus that the disappearance of their boss became evident.*

*"He was here a minute ago," said Pete. "Hard to keep track of him. It's like he can walk through walls. Always vanishing. Why don't ya call Martha, his personal assistant, and set up an appointment for some time next week, Mr.—?"*

*"Patterson. But that won't work," the man said. "I really need to see him today.* <u>Now</u>. *Can you locate him, maybe call his cell phone?"*

*"He doesn't carry one," said Matt. "He just kind of knows when we need him. Maybe we can help you."*

*"I appreciate that, but no," insisted the man. "It has to be him."*

*"We have to meet with the boss in about half an hour," said Matt, "to go over the plans for how this new building will be laid out and* <u>what</u> *will go* <u>where</u> *inside, once it's constructed. We've got a work tent set up. But it's just for those of us on the leadership team. Sorry. However, if you give me your contact information, I'll relay...."*

*"Where is this meeting? What tent? Where is it?"*

*Pete took a step forward. "Uh-uh, compadre. It's off limits. We got a ton of work to do, so there won't be any private meetings today with the boss. Just call next week and.... "*

*"You don't understand! I'm not asking for myself. It's crucial we see Jesus today."*

"We?" echoed Matt. "You're not alone?"

"There are five of us," said the man, lifting his hand in a vague wave of direction. "It's a long story, but the bottom line is this. A year ago we were army scouts on patrol in Afghanistan, making sure the trek through a certain valley would be safe for our follow-up vehicles. We got caught in an ambush. Our sarge, Billy Ray Jackson, drew fire while the rest of us ran for cover. He took some shrapnel in his legs. We got him out eventually, but he hasn't walked since. Therapy doesn't seem to be working, or the splints or the drugs or baths. The sarge…he's just given up."

"Real sorry about your pal, but we ain't runnin' no hospital," said Pete.

"He doesn't need a hospital," said the stranger. "He needs a will to live. My buddies and I read some stories online about how Jesus hires people everyone else has cast aside. He gives them training, responsibility, personal dignity. They get a chance at a new life. It's miraculous. And that's what our friend needs—a miracle. Just give us half an hour. I know it'll make a world of difference. What do you say?"

Matt shook his head. "We do hire people who are physically challenged, but not today. We've got a jam-packed agenda we have to go over this afternoon. Bring your friend around sometime next week and go to our personnel director. She'll see what we may have open."

Patterson stood rigid, angrily flexing his fingers. "What part of 'we owe this guy our lives' are you not understanding?

"We get it," said Pete, "but ya come to us on the wrong day. Bring your friend back next week."

From a few yards away Sy Zylotski yelled, "Hey, you guys, get over here and plant your feet with us."

"Sorry," Pete said to Patterson, "but we gotta go. Like I said, bring your friend in next week."

Pete and Matt left the man and advanced to a plot of wet concrete that had just been smoothed by workmen.

"Okay, take off your shoes, Gents, and squish your feet into this stuff before it starts to harden. One small step for man.... " Sy set the example by slipping off his flip-flops and stepping into the concrete. He moved back, then leaned over and used his forefinger to scrawl his name next to the imprint of his feet. "Hey, anybody bring some washcloths or towels?"

"Just walk through the grass on the way to the work tent," said Matt. "It'll probably rub off."

One by one the execs made the imprints of their feet and wrote their names. Then, to explain to future generations the symbolism of the footprints, Matt wrote "Taking Steps Forward" across the top. As the execs made their way from the dedication area to a group of large shade trees where the work tent had been set up, Matt nodded over his shoulder and Pete turned to look. Patterson was still watching where they were going.

"Persistent, ain't he?" said Pete.

When the men arrived at the work tent, they were surprised to see Jesus blocking the entrance.

*"You're not coming in like that," Jesus stated. "Sit on these side benches and let me clean you."*

*The men weren't quite certain what he meant. Jesus reached back into the tent, extracted a bucket of soapy water, and also retrieved some towels, which he draped over his shoulders. "I said to sit. I'm going to wash your hands and feet."*

*Genuinely appalled, Pete said, "You gotta be jokin', Boss. If there's any washin' to do, it should be done by an old roughneck like me."*

*Jesus shook his head and smiled. "I've been busy cleaning you up since the day we met. Why should today be any different?"*

*Pete considered that a moment, then laughed. "Can't argue with that, Boss. Okay, in that case, give me a full once-over. Be sure to check behind my ears." All of the men chuckled, and a few punched Pete in the shoulder or ruffled his hair on their way past as they dropped onto the ground or sat on a couple of weather-beaten sets of bleachers. One by one, they allowed Jesus to wipe the caked concrete from their feet and hands. Most felt self-conscious about being washed up by the boss, but they had learned long ago to obey the man, no matter how bizarre his requests might be. Sooner or later, the situation would make sense.*

*"There's a lesson here," Jesus announced.*

*"Yep," said Pete in a low voice. "There usually is . . . and, most likely, we won't get it."*

*"Service is more important than products,"* Jesus continued. *"When people come to us with needs, we are never too proud, too busy, or too preoccupied to show compassion and care. We exalt our character through humility. We turn no one away."*

*Pete and Matt looked at each other. Simultaneously they murmured, "Uh-oh."*

*"Let's go inside," said Jesus. "We have a lot of work to do. I want everything to be clear in your minds as to how to carry on once I turn everything over to you."*

*Judas held back a moment and waved an arm, summoning Jonathan. The younger man, who had been visiting with some of the other employees after he'd finished his photography obligations, saw the wave and hustled across the yard to where Judas stood.*

*"You need me for something, sir?"*

*"Yes," said Judas, lowering his voice slightly. "We're going into this tent to study some blueprints and to lay out some plans for the company's expansion. It's not often that we can corner Jesus long enough to get work like this done, although, goodness knows, I'm continually trying."*

*Jonathan nodded vigorously. "You are that, sir. No denying."*

*Judas paused a few seconds to see if there was sarcasm is the young man's voice. He let it go.*

*"If I know this crowd—and I do—there are going to be people wandering over here trying to get personal time with*

*Jesus. We can't allow that. These expansion plans are too important. I want you to get five or six of the fellows from second shift to sort of stand guard over here. No rough stuff, of course, but just make sure that no one gets into this tent. I'll authorize overtime, if need be. But remember, no one—and I mean <u>no one</u>—enters this tent until we've finished our meeting."*

*"Sure, I can handle that," said Jonathan. "I know just the guys for the job. I'll be back in five minutes. Go ahead and start your meeting. I'll make sure you're not disturbed."*

*Judas smiled, very pleased. "Excellent. Thank you." He turned and hurried into the tent. He wanted to make sure he was in on every detail of how the company could expand its operations, and, hence, its profits. "Foot washings...exaltation through humility," he mused. "In what MBA program did he come up with that stuff?"*

*True to his word, within a few minutes Jonathan had returned with a cadre of coworkers who spaced themselves around the tent's entrance flap, forming a human barrier. And, indeed, as Judas had predicted, many folks who had attended the groundbreaking and dedication started looking in various places to see if Jesus was present. A sizeable cluster approached the tent, but Jonathan stepped out and raised an open flat hand.*

*"Sorry, folks, but this is as far as you can go."*

*Various voices arose with calls of, "We're looking for Jesus" and "Is Jesus in that tent?" and "Someone saw Jesus here earlier, and we'd like to talk with him." Again Jonathan held back the crowd and explained that there would be no private meetings with Jesus.*

*"So, you're saying that Jesus is, indeed, inside that tent?" asked one man, moving close to the front of the crowd.*

*Jonathan stared at the man. He had seen him earlier, standing with Pete and Matt.*

*"Yes, sir, but he's conducting an important business meeting right now. We can't allow anyone to disturb him." Jonathan nodded toward several burly factory workers who flanked him.*

*The man assessed the situation and did not try to force an entry. Instead, he wandered first left, then right, then left again, studying the tent's tarp, support ropes, and pegs, along with the large shade trees that flanked the tent's back and sides. His eyes were those of a trained scout, someone who knew how to survey a situation quickly and devise either a retreat or an attack. Then he turned, made his way through the crowd, and crossed the field again.*

*The next half hour passed uneventfully, save for the fact that the sun was relentless and Jonathan and his cohorts wished the tent meeting would end so that they could head home. The waiting crowd had not disbursed, but neither had anyone caused a ruckus. Most seemed content to wait, hoping to see Jesus and call out to him once he left the tent. In time, Jonathan and his companions sat on the ground, still watchful of the tent door, but not as vigilant as when the crowd had first assembled.*

*Meanwhile, unbeknownst to those guarding the tent's entrance, a stealthy group of military stalkers was making its way to the rear of the tent. Four men carried someone on a green stretcher, the kind often used in field evacuations in military zones. They moved forward in unison quicksteps, halting at the back of the tent and easing the man to the ground. Wordlessly, the two men in front pulled off measures of thick rope from around their chests.*

*"Up you go," said the leader.*

*"Okay, Patterson," said one of the men in front as he and his buddy rapidly moved to the trunk of the nearest large shade tree and climbed to the lowest branches.*

*Patterson grabbed the two coils of thick rope, went to the tree and tossed them to the two men, who then climbed high above. He then took the ends of the ropes and attached them to the front of the stretcher. Methodically, he attached two other coils of rope to the back. "Hang on, Sarge. You're going for a little ride," he told the man lying on the stretcher. "We've got you strapped in. You'll be fine." He nodded to another man, and the two of them, ropes cinched around their waists, climbed a second tree. With a nod, Patterson signaled it was time to start slowly raising their comrade.*

*Suspended on the ropes and dangling between the two large trees, the stretcher left the ground and was maneuvered* directly above the large work tent. Jonathan and the men guarding the tent's front entrance were still seated on the ground with their backs to the action.

However, some folks in the gathered crowd began to point and talk.

When the stretcher was poised directly above the tent, Patterson attached a pulley to his section of rope and glided through the air until he reached Billy Ray. Hooking his legs to the thick rope, Patterson suspended himself upside down, extracted a huge knife from his utility belt, and stabbed the top of the tent, tearing away pieces of the canvas.

By now, Jonathan and the other security workers were on their feet and running to the back of the tent. But there were no ladders. They had no way of getting to where the invaders had positioned themselves.

Inside the tent, Matt, Pete, Sy, and Nate were forming a protective human wall around Jesus, not sure what was going on. Above them, Patterson righted himself on the thick rope and flashed a thumbs-up signal to his teammates. He steadied the stretcher as the others lessened the tension on the ropes and allowed it to descend inside the tent.

"We mean no harm," Patterson called out. "No need to be scared. Don't be alarmed."

Jesus stepped forward, edging past his would-be protectors. "I'm not alarmed," he said. "I'm not even surprised." He looked at Judas. "Go outside and have Jonathan bring the other men in to join their friends, please."

"But this is an outrage," Judas protested. "We should call the police. This is destruction of private property, invasion of..."

Jesus raised a hand. "Please! My will be done. Bring the other men to me."

Judas glared hard but finally turned and walked toward the tent flat.

"Oh...and Judas," Jesus added as something of an afterthought. "Be careful around those ropes."

Judas paused, pondered the comment, then exited the tent shaking his head. "I'll never understand him," he murmured.

"Untie your friend," Jesus instructed Patterson. "Matt, some water for our visitors, please."

As Patterson hastily pulled the Velcro straps from around Billy Ray, he began to babble. "I tried...we tried earlier to talk to you...I'm sorry about this, but...see, my friend here...."

Jesus ignored him. He reached out a hand and helped Billy Ray rise to a sitting position, then he knelt. "Your friends care very deeply about you," said Jesus. "They've gone to a lot of trouble to bring you to me. A greater question is, are you ready to come to me?"

Haggard lines across Billy Ray's forehead and in his cheeks evidenced premature aging brought on by stress and anxiety. Although no more than thirty-five, his hair was going *gray, his eyes were sunken, and the pallor of his skin indicated his struggle with an inner sickness.*

*"Colors," he said. "Can't escape the colors since the war."*

*His three other friends entered the tent and moved near Billy Ray, Patterson, and Jesus.*

*"Tell me about the colors," said Jesus.*

*Slowly, Billy Ray lowered his eyes and shook his head slightly. "Red all over my hands...*black all around my heart...*gray all over the bodies of the enemy...."*

*"He says stuff like that," said one of the men. "Docs can't help him. They got no idea what he's talking about."*

*Gently, Jesus lifted the man's chin and looked him straight in the eyes. "Though your sins be as scarlet, I will make them as white as snow. I'll give you a new color."*

*Billy Ray squinted but didn't turn his head. "It...it wasn't the war, was it?"*

*"No," said Jesus. "You did your duty. You went to the war to try to forget your other failures. You had the colors before you ever entered combat, didn't you?"*

*A tear coursed its way down the man's cheek. "I've been sick a long time. Heartsick. Homesick. Guilty. No one understands."*

*"I do. There's more than one battlefield in life. You wounded others. You know who you've hurt and what needs to be done to provide a cure. Get off this cot, go home, and make*

*amends. Heal those you've hurt, and I promise you, you'll be healed, too."*

*Jesus stood and waved his arms to make everyone move back. "Let him stand on his own two feet. He's ready to start healing."*

*Patterson looked dubiously at Jesus. "But the doctors told us...."*

*Slowly, heavily, Billy Ray moved to one knee and then struggled into a standing position. He gained his bearings and looked at Jesus. "Thank you," he said. "Thank you." He looked at his friends and the others in the tent before turning his attention back to Jesus. "I know what I need to do." He took two steps toward the exit flap, but Jesus grabbed his arm.*

*"Wait," Jesus said. "Roll up the stretcher. Take it with you. Put it someplace where you'll see it every day. Don't regress."*

*Billy Ray stopped. "Yeah, good idea." Before retrieving the stretcher, he waited a moment in thought, then straightened himself into his best sergeant posture and said, "Troops, attention!" The other four men instinctively snapped to attention. "Salute!" The five men raised their arms in a salute of respect to Jesus.*

*"You would have made a great battlefield commander, sir," said Sergeant Jackson.*

*Jesus looked back wryly and said softly, "My day is coming."*

# Section *10*

## LESSONS FROM SUBMARINE PEOPLE

Submarines will sink deeper and deeper the more dead weight (ballast) they take on. In order to rise, break through the surface, and ride on the high crest, the submarine must jettison the ballast. People are the same way. However, even if we manage to jettison the dead weight from our lives, too often we allow it to seep back in, and we end up sinking to levels even lower than we once had been. Let me offer some examples.

As I mentioned in section 3, an average Joe will win the lottery and be handed two million dollars. He's set for life, got it made. Yet, you check back with him three years later, and you discover the money is gone. All of it. The guy is back working at the factory. What in the world happened?

A heart attack victim will work with a trainer and a dietician for a year, and she will drop 125 pounds. She is in better health than ever. She looks good, feels good, and has more energy, more vitality, and more self-respect than at any time in her life. Yet, follow up on her three years later, and she will have gained back the entire 125 pounds, plus added fifteen more. How can this be?

A family of hoarders will have its property condemned by the city. In sympathy, a team of professional organizers will come in and remove the clutter and debris. They will wash and neatly arrange everything in the whole house. They'll set up systems so the family members can be safe, healthy, and systematic in all they do. But if the organizers come back in a year, they'll discover the house has become a dump again. Windows are grimy, carpets are stained, appliances are broken, and garbage is piled at the back door.

How did so much, go so wrong, in so short a time? Indeed…*why*?

Why do some people rise to the surface, break free of the ocean of negativity, and ride the crest, whereas others rise to the surface, temporarily hold their positions, and then slowly sink back into the murky, dark depths of failure? The answer is quite basic: some people are able to gain a long-range vision of personal success that becomes self-motivating and self-sustaining; others, however, are able to excel only for a season before recalling negative memories of past failures and reverting to previously established bad habits.

We can learn five valuable lessons by examining the two different types of submarine people.

**Lesson One: Some people realize that before they can rise and stay at new levels, they first must change their behavior patterns.**

A man prayed every day for a month for God to let him win the lottery. It didn't happen. At the end of the month the man protested, "God, I've prayed diligently for weeks on end to win the lottery. Why have you not answered my prayer?" God replied, "Do *your* part, Bob. Go buy a ticket."

Indeed, a steam locomotive will pull for you, but only if you first shovel in the coal. A cell phone will carry a message for you, but only if you first erect the relay towers. A book will give you knowledge, but only if you turn its pages and read its words. You have to do your part.

It is God's practice to prepare his servants for the time of his calling. As I noted in the fourth section of this book, Noah and his sons worked for decades building the ark. In the process, they served as warning agents of all who could yet choose to repent and follow a life of obedience to God. Joshua served forty years as the assistant to Moses before assuming command of the Jewish exiles. Because of his loyalty, God granted him a long life wherein he would fulfill a destiny of his own. Elisha served under Elijah, Samuel served under Eli, and the disciples served under

Jesus. God expects us to spend time in development so that we can do more for him, for others, and for ourselves.

I once interviewed the successful novelist and short story writer Harry Mark Petrakis for a feature story in a writer's magazine. In 1966 his novel *A Dream of Kings* became a blockbuster best-seller, and in 1969 it became a popular movie starring Anthony Quinn and Irene Papas. Petrakis told me that he knew in his twenties he wanted to be a professional writer one day. He used to go to public libraries and just rub his hands over the cover of books, touching the bindings, smelling the ink, caressing the pages. To Petrakis, being the author of a book was the ultimate in achievement, the epitome of artistic mastery.

Petrakis set out to become a book writer. He read books on writing. He practiced writing. He talked to other writers and questioned them. But he had no success. For a decade he held part-time jobs while continuing to write and send out manuscripts. Success as an author eluded him. Near the end of a decade of honing his craft he wrote a short story titled, "Pericles on 31$^{st}$ Street." With grand bravado he submitted it to the prestigious *Atlantic Monthly*. It was accepted as an "Atlantic First" story, meaning it was a debut of a promising new writer. Subsequently, the screen rights were purchased, and it was made into a teleplay for *The Dick Powell Theatre*.

In time, Petrakis wrote more short stories, then novels and nonfiction books, and ultimately scripts, too. He won numerous awards and became very wealthy and was a popular speaker at writers' conferences. He told me in that interview, "Not one day of that ten-year apprenticeship was wasted. Every book read, every manuscript typed, every writing lesson gleaned from other writers all combined to make me the writer I ultimately became. There is a price to pay for artistic achievement, and I was willing to pay it."

Famed guitarist Chet Atkins told me a similar story. When I interviewed him in 1969 for a national magazine, Chet took down a guitar and played a new piece he was working on. It was magic the way his fingers flew across those strings, agilely firing off riffs of sixteenth notes, plucking phenomenal string blendings of unique harmonics, and blitzing through melodies so complicated I could barely comprehend the range of tones. He made it all look so easy, so natural.

When he finished, I sat in awe, my mouth hanging open. Finally, I said, "Wow! I would give anything to be able to play like that." Chet smiled wryly and said, "No, you wouldn't. You see, I gave *everything* in order to play like that." He talked about practicing the guitar and the fiddle when other kids played ball or worked summer jobs or attended parties. He talked about practicing late into the night, early in the morning, on weekdays and weekends. It took decades of rehearsing, exploring, experimenting, practicing, and implementing before he reached such a state of excellence as a musician that he became a world famous recording artist and someone who performed with great orchestras across America.

What we draw from this first lesson is, the degree to which you wish to experience success will be determined by the amount of effort you are willing to commit to your development. Some people read books, listen to lectures, study magazines, travel to interesting places, attend seminars, and participate in workshops. Other people play video games, watch sporting events, take naps, watch movies, and work at non-challenging occupations. In short, there are people who make advances in life, and there are those who go through the motions. Anyone who does not change negative behavior patterns to reflect an aggressively positive way of life will eventually sink to new lows.

## Lesson Two: Some people know when they have been blessed, whereas other people fear gifts from God.

We all are familiar with instances in the Bible when God wanted to bless people, but they squelched the blessing. As we've noted before, God promised to make Moses a great orator before Pharaoh, but Moses was scared and hesitant, so, instead, God gave the oratory gift to Aaron. Samson misused the gift of physical strength; Balaam misused his priestly power of blessing and anointing; Ananias and Sapphira misused the blessing of financial substance.

Perhaps you can identify with these people. Perhaps you genuinely feel that the Lord has been calling you to use your gifts to impact the world in a significant way. Maybe it's even more serious than that. Maybe you are terrified that because you are turning a blind eye and a deaf ear to God's calling, he will do to you what he did to Moses—he will retract the blessing and withdraw the gifts and call someone else to do what you have been afraid to do.

If this is your situation, let me offer some words of encouragement.

- First, just by reading this book, you have taken a bold step forward. You've committed time, money, and effort toward exploring *specific* ways both to advance and to enhance your skills. Well done!

- Second, you now can redirect your focus toward better biblical models. Gideon was absolutely stunned when the angel of the Lord called him to become military commander of the Jewish army, but in faith he rose to the challenge and was successful. Isaiah declared himself to be a man of unclean lips, unworthy of God's call to be a prophet, but he rose to the challenge and fulfilled the calling. David was a fifth the height and weight of Goliath, but he attacked the giant anyway. The apostle Paul called himself "the chief of sinners," yet he put that behind him and "pressed forward for the high calling of Christ."

It's okay to be a bit scared...to be dazzled...to be humbled. Get in line! Many have been there before you, and they rose to do great deeds. So *can* you, so *will* you! Just remember that you must accept a blessing and not fear a gift from God.

**Lesson Three: Some people think they can tread water, whereas other people know they can stay afloat only if they keep moving forward.**

When I worked my way through college playing in a five-piece combo and teaching guitar lessons at a music store, for a time I thought I might make music my career. I was good, very good. But an incident during my teen years made me change my mind.

My brother Gary and I had written some country music songs. We went into a small studio in our home state of Michigan and cut six demos, then drove to Nashville and started making the rounds of major recording companies to pitch our songs. Although we didn't make any sales that trip (years later I had better results in selling some gospel tunes I wrote), we had a chance to listen in on some recording sessions.

I was flabbergasted by the talent of the amazing session musicians. Yet, they weren't stars in their own right. They just sat by the phone each day and hoped their union rep would call and say they were needed for a session. On rare occasions one of these "sidemen," such as Jerry Reed, Barbara Mandrell, James Burton, or Glen Campbell, would emerge as a solo act. But for each breakout artist, there were seven hundred master musicians who continued to work for scale and remained anonymous. Curious about this situation, I questioned some of the sidemen about what it took to break out. What they shared with me had applications to my development as a writer, as a public orator, and as a college professor.

One pianist said, "I'm one of the best sight readers anywhere. Put a sheet of music in front of me, and I can play it to perfection within minutes. But that's all I do. I play *other* people's music. I've never composed anything original. I'm a reader, not a composer or writer."

A guitarist in his mid-twenties told me, "I've hung around country pickers all my life—barn dances, honky-tonks, jamborees. I know every lick and chord from Hank Williams to Buck Owens. Trouble is, that's the extent of my range. I don't know jazz riffs. I've never mastered flamenco finger-style playing. I couldn't play a classical number to save my life. I'm the best at what I do, but what I do is just one slice of the musical pie. As a result, I miss out on a lot of work."

239

Jesus in All Four Seasons

An older fellow who played standing bass told me, "I've always made a basic living by being flexible and content. If someone needed a bass player and background singer for a three-month road tour, I'd sign on. If a local radio station needed a bass player for a Sunday morning gospel hour, I'd take the job. I'd do session work, fill in at bars, whatever was available. Trouble was, I never became a specialist. I never developed a unique style, an original sound. I was content to earn a paycheck by being 'good enough.' I was adequate, not distinctive."

Today, after having met many people in all walks of life and in a vast array of professions, I see parallels between those talented but unfulfilled musicians and people with similar constrictions. Even in my own field of writing, there are vast numbers of sidemen—reporters for modest circulation newspapers, poets who've been published only in obscure literary quarterlies, playwrights whose works have never made it past the school or church stage, English teachers who are still working on those novels started back in college. They all fantasize about hitting the *New York Times* best-seller list, winning a Pulitzer Prize, getting a screen adaptation offer from Steven Spielberg, and being profiled in *Writer's Digest*. So, why isn't it happening? And why isn't it happening for people in other lines of work? Well, actually, for identical reasons as the sidemen musicians.

Like the piano player, many would-be writers, inventors, composers, and entrepreneurs spend their prime-time hours reading other people's success stories rather than creating their own. Yes, reading is critical to the development of any successful person. But successful people must work. Striving for balance is crucial.

Like the guitarist, many new artists, directors, athletes, and executives limit their development by exploring one medium or one venue *ad infinitum*. Highly successful people understand the value of dominance in an arena of competition, but they also understand the necessity of diversity of skills. They are constantly reinventing themselves in more and more expansive ways. The wider a person's range of talents, the greater the amount of work he or she will generate. Thus, to amplify one's talents is to amplify one's success.

And like the bass player, too many fledgling designers, politicians, scientists, and performers waste time dabbling rather than focusing. Sure, as novices we're willing to take on any assignment or task offered to us. That's survival. However, it's not progress. To advance, we must master a skill set, gain a reputation and following, and then move to new levels of expertise, always securing our clientele based on genuine talent and knowledge.

Sidemen sit on the sides. They supplement the stars. The stars stand out. They are the soloists. For you, it's a decision and a process. You can become a maestro, or you can remain a second fiddle.

## Lesson Four: Some people realize that staying on top is a team effort and not always a solo endeavor.

The captain of a submarine can get his sub to the surface, but to keep the sub on track, the captain needs the help of a navigator, a communications officer, a sonar and radar specialist, a meteorologist, and a maintenance crew. In like manner, each of us needs a support team.

I know of two women who are both successful editors of popular magazines. They have been meeting for dinner once a month for more than twenty years. When they meet, they catch up on social news, but then the conversation turns more specific. They ask each other about their editing projects, their deadlines, their own personal writing endeavors, their current reading, their prayer needs, their health, their finances, and their long and short term goals. They remind each other of promises they have made, desires they have expressed, and dreams they have yet to fulfill. They make suggestions, share insights and ideas, and pledge to be supportive, even if it means an occasional admonition. This sort of camaraderie helps keep their feet to the fire. It motivates them to want to have something positive to report on each month. It gives them a sounding board. They create a synergy when they're together, and each leaves the meeting a better person for having invested in the other.

Many folks have heard of the Algonquin Roundtable of 1919 in New York City, wherein such literary giants as Edna Ferber, Dorothy Parker, George S. Kaufman, Alexander Woollcott, Robert Benchley, and even Harpo Marx gathered each day for lunch and repartee. Although they usually gossiped, joked, and shared barbs about Broadway shows or new restaurants, the fact is, many of them also used this time to discuss their current writing projects. They put forth ideas and listened to feedback, criticism, and suggestions. To the outside world, this was a gathering of elitist critics and snobbish members of the literati, but in reality, these hard-working writers didn't have time to be frivolous in wasting an hour or two every day. No, they were using one another in a somewhat biblical practice of iron sharpening iron in making their own writings as razor-edged as possible. The lesson we can learn from these master writers is that it's wise for us to have talented, experienced, insightful, creative, and perceptive accountability partners, no matter what line of work or career development we are pursuing. Even the Lone Ranger had Tonto.

## Lesson Five: When riding the crest, be vigilant about expecting an enemy attack.

An enemy can come at you in stealth mode and attack you before you realize it. You may become the victim of failure, exhaustion, rejection, confusion, depression, or fatigue. Instead of letting that happen, anticipate such attacks and prepare to deal with them.

When I was a soldier, I learned a very important lesson about this. I spent the first year of my enlistment as a member of the United States Army Armor Corps. We were the sons of Patton. After a year in Armor, I began to think I was John Wayne and Rambo rolled into one. I was invincible, vicious, badder than bad.

At the end of 1970, I was transferred to Vietnam. Since that was a jungle war and tanks were not in high demand there, I was assigned to the military police as a chaplain's bodyguard. I left America on December 28. The entire time I was flying across the Pacific Ocean, I kept thinking, *All right! About time they sent for me. Let's wrap this thing up!* Now, here was a twenty-two-year-old kid from Michigan who had never even seen a jungle except in a Tarzan movie, but I was ready to go over there and wrap up this war for our country.

We arrived on January 2, 1971. When I had left Detroit days earlier, the temperature had been three degrees. When we landed at Tan Son Nhat airport, outside of Saigon, it was 103 degrees. Military leaders had all 160 men on that flight fall out and line up in four rows of forty in each row. We stood at attention for more than half an hour, dripping sweat. Finally, from a distant metal hut emerged a tall, lanky first sergeant. His sun-bleached uniform was a sure sign he had been in Vietnam at least a year or two. But the faded uniform was starched and creased, his boots were spit-shined, and he wore his combat helmet exactly two fingers above the bridge of his nose. This guy was *strack*. You couldn't get any more serious about being military than he was.

The first sergeant said nothing. He just walked up and down those rows of men, looking us up and down, up and down. Finally, he came back to the number-one man in the number one row, which, just by the fool luck of how we had come out of that airplane, was *me*.

He scrutinized me thoroughly, then peered at the name on my breastplate. "Hens-LEE! Hens-LEE!" he shouted.

Without averting my eyes, I responded in an equally loud voice, "Yes, First Sergeant!"

He looked me up and down a few more times, and then he leaned in close and said, "You are mean, tough, and ornery, aren't you, boy?"

And I thought, *What an amazing judge of character this man is.*

I replied, "I *am* mean, tough, and ornery, First Sergeant!"

He nodded, then said, "You're ready to end this war all by yourself, aren't you, boy?"

I concurred. "I *am* ready to end this war all by myself, First Sergeant!"

"Yeah, yeah," he said. "What you're really ready to do is go home tomorrow morning in a body bag, that's what *you're* ready to do."

This baffled me. Couldn't he see the insignia on my arm that indicated I was coming from the Armor Corps? Didn't he realize I was the meanest of the mean, the toughest of the tough?

But then he did something that caught me completely by surprise. He leaned close, within two inches of my face, and he began to sniff me. *Sniff…sniff…sniffffffff.* "What is that, boy?" he roared.

Without hesitation I said, "English Leather, First Sergeant."

"English Leather," he said. "English Leather." He started to pound his forefinger into my chest and asked, "How many of Charlie Cong's boys do you think are out there in the jungle today wearing English Leather, tough-guy Hens-LEE?"

I thought about that for about three seconds, and then mumbled, "Probably…uh, probably none, First Sergeant?"

"That's ri-*ight*," he affirmed, giving *right* two syllables. He pounded my chest again and asked, "So, if you go on patrol tonight and they smell that on the wind, who's coming, our boys or theirs?"

I gulped. "I...I guess that would be us, First Sergeant."

He grinned dourly and said, "Exactly. And so, they will just crouch inside the tall grass and wait for you to walk down the trail, and then they will blow your head off. I *wouldn't wear* cologne in the jungle if I were you, tough-guy Hens-LEE!"

Oh, my gosh. The temperature was more than a hundred degrees, but my knees started to knock together. It was suddenly dawning on me that those people in that jungle were going to spend the next year doing everything possible to kill me, and the only thing preventing that from happening was this man in front of me. I started to listen to him—not figuratively, but literally—for dear life.

For the next twenty minutes he explained to everyone in earshot what a complete idiot I was. He screamed at me for wearing a luminous dial watch because the enemy could see that half a mile away at night. He screamed at me for not having a completely bald head so as to keep myself clean and lice-free. On and on he ranted, going from the top of my head to the bottom of my feet, explained a dozen reasons why I was going to die that very day if I didn't shut up and listen to everything he had to say.

That wasn't going to be a problem. Scared out of my wits, I listened to everything he had to say and burned it into my memory. I was too terrified to be embarrassed at being his poster child for combat ineptitude.

Finally, he stepped back from me and yelled out to everyone, "I'm not picking on ol' Hens-LEE, here. He's no worse off than the rest of you clowns. He just happened to be handy."

He strode back to front and center and uttered words that would change my life forever. He said, "This is what it comes down to, gentlemen: If *you* know *your enemy* better than your enemy knows *you*, then one year from today you will go home looking the way you look now. However, if your enemy knows *you* better than you know *your enemy*, then you are going to lose. And trust me, gentlemen, you do *not* want to lose over here."

He paused momentarily and then added, "And this applies to everything you will ever do, even when you get back to the States. If you go to college on the GI Bill and everyone else is making excellent grades and winning scholarships except you, that situation is *the enemy.* You'd better find out all you can about the enemy. What extra books could you be reading? How much time should you be spending in the laboratory? Who can you get to tutor you in your hardest subjects?"

He continued, "If you get a job and everyone else is getting promotions and raises but not you, that situation is *the enemy.* You'd better find out all you can about the enemy. Who can I get to mentor me in this line of work?

How much overtime should I be putting in to set a good example? What seminars could I enroll in to help me learn more about my trade and craft?"

I freely confess that although I have earned four university degrees, I have never received better advice. Now, many decades later, I can still hear that man's voice echoing those admonitions in my ear. As a result, I continue to study. I continue to stay current in my field. I continue to watch my blind side. I'm always anticipating enemy attacks and thwarting them. You can and should do likewise.

**All Hands on Deck**

After identifying the five strategies used by submarine people who rise to the top and stay on top, we can use those strategies to our advantage by changing our behavior, knowing when we've been blessed, moving forward continually, staying on top through a team effort, and being vigilant against enemy attack. Then, if we sink, it's our own fault.

So, jettison the ballast, rise to the surface, keep moving forward, and stay the course.

## Key Points Found in Section *10*

1. It's not enough to rise to the surface. Without determination and a plan, you will slowly sink back into the waters of defeat.

2. To rise and stay at new levels, it is necessary to jettison former bad habits and to stay aligned with new, positive habits.

3. When given a gift or blessing from God, make use of it lest it be taken from you.

4. Treading water gets you nowhere. You must keep moving forward in order to stay afloat.

5. Staying on top is best done with help from accountability partners, teachers, mentors, and coaches. Make it a team effort, not a solo act.

6. Once on top, expect an enemy attack. Be vigilant, prepared, and resourceful. Don't allow anything or anyone to thwart your progress.

*Two sharp raps on his office door frame caused Jesus to look up from the paperwork before him.*

*"Jimmy!" Jesus pushed back his chair, came around the desk, and heartily hugged his brother.*

*"I've missed you. Come for a job?"*

*It was a long standing joke between them.*

*"Not yet. It was hard enough growing up in your shadow. Mom still tells the story of the time when you were twelve and you got sent to the principal's office for correcting your teacher in geography class. Turns out, you were right." He shook a finger. "Wise guy."*

*Jesus ruffled his brother's hair and they shared a laugh. Jimmy dropped into a chair.*

*Jesus casually eased back against his desk. A moment of silence passed, then Jesus said, "She sent you?"*

*"Yeah. Of course. You need to come home." Worry creased his face. "Dad's dying. He's proud of you, proud of what you're doing. He'd never send for you, but Mom...."*

*"I understand." Jesus smiled. "She's always been strong-willed. Did I ever tell you about the time she came to our company picnic and we ran out of soft drinks? She came tromping over to me...."*

*Jimmy lifted a hand. "Yep, I was there. She's no respecter of persons when she feels she's in the right." He* hunched forward slightly. "That's why she sent me to bring you home. She wants you to…to, uh, <u>help</u> Dad."

"Is that what he wants?"

Jimmy shook his head. "You know Dad. It's all about us, never about him. He always made us feel special. You are special, Bro', but none of us ever felt he loved any one of us more than the others. I'm really going to miss him. Still, Dad understands when…."

Jesus nodded. "Sure he does. But Mom won't be ready to give him up. We're going to have to convince her we'll always be there to take care of her."

"So, you'll come with me?"

"Naturally. But I want to bring someone with me. You know John Brothers, the young guy on my staff?"

"Yeah, yeah, I've met him. Nice guy. Why do we need him?"

"I trust him. Professionally and personally. He's not a relative, but I've come to love him like a family member. He's low key, but dependable. If I can't—<u>when</u> I can't—be there for Mom, he'll cover for me."

Jimmy looked grim. "You can still call this off. There's time. You've already done a lot. Your legacy will live on."

Jesus moved closer and put an arm around his younger brother's shoulder. "It isn't about leaving a legacy, Jimmy. It's about changing lives. Come on. We'll grab John on our way out."

*The family home hadn't changed much since Jesus and Jimmy were boys. Mary hurried outside and met them.*

*"You're here," she said, and moved into the arms of Jesus. "You're finally here."*

*"I am with you always, Mom. You know that."*

*She looked up into her son's eyes.*

*"He's bad off. He needs help I can't provide. Go to him. Help him. You do what's right."*

*"I will do <u>what's right</u>, Mom. You need to believe that."*

*Mary squeezed her son fiercely. "I love him. I need him. He stood by me when everyone called me...."*

*Jesus put a finger to his mother's lips. "Shh...shhhh. I know all about that. That was a long time ago."*

*"No," she countered. "Not so long ago. Some wounds heal, maybe, but scars remain. Others may doubt, but me—I know. I hope you'll never have to know about bearing such scars."*

*For a moment Jesus merely returned his mother's embrace. Finally, he softly whispered, "Don't dwell on that," and eased himself free of her grip. "I'll see Dad now. Alone."*

*He entered the house and moved down the hall. He opened the bedroom door without knocking. His father,*

*Joseph, lay motionless, his breathing shallow, his face drained of color, his hair and beard gray but neatly trimmed by a wife who continued to preserve his dignity.*

*Jesus pulled a cushioned chair to the side of the bed. "I'm here, Pop."*

*The old man's eyelids flitted, then opened to slits. He said calmly, "So you are." He smiled slightly. "She gets her way, doesn't she? Sorry to annoy you, Son. I told her you'd know when it was time, and you'd come."*

*"That's...exactly...right."*

*Joseph weighed that briefly, then sighed.*

*"Ah, well, I see. Then so be it." He turned his head ever so slightly. "Give me your hands. Both hands."*

*Obediently, Jesus stretched forth his hands and gently rested them atop his father's chest. Eagerly, the older man used his fingers as eyes, probing his son's wrists, knuckles, palms, and fingers.*

*"Good boy, good boy," he said, wheezing. "Calluses. Small cuts. Strong muscles. You're still working with the wood, aren't you? That's my boy. Good, good."*

*"You taught me well, Pop. No matter how many demands people put on us, we still need to have an opportunity to think and meditate. Do something physical. It's great for restoring the soul."*

*"And if you wind up with a new set of bookshelves in the process, so much the better, eh?"*

"There's also that," Jesus agreed, smiling. A moment passed, then softly he squeezed Joseph's hands. "I love you, Dad."

Tears formed in the old man's eyes. They rolled down the sides of his face. "Such a good boy. Always such a good boy." Again there was a silent pause.

"I owe you so much, Dad, that I feel obligated...."

"Stop!" The rebuttal was strong for one so weak. "There is a time to be born and a time to die. It's fair. It's just. If any man has enjoyed a full life, it is this man." He paused in reflection. "I have seen miracles. I have been blessed enough. But I have one more lesson to teach you."

Jesus leaned closer so that his father could sense his attentiveness.

"We know what lies ahead for you," he said, barely above a whisper. "If I could take your place, I would. But that is not to be. So, instead, I want you to watch me now. Observe me closely. My hands are old, but tonight they do not shake. My body is feeble, but my mind is clear and sharp. Can you see this?"

"I can, Pop, truly I can."

"So...you will see me face death with no fear, no hesitation. It pleases me to have you at my side."

The old man groped until he found his son's hands again. He held them with passion.

"When that dreadful day comes, you think back to tonight. You remember your beloved Papa, and you be strong.

*Like me, you <u>choose</u> the time to die. Remember this night. Remember me."*

*Jesus shifted and gripped the elderly man's shoulder. "I will, Pop. I'll remember. And I promise you, I won't give up until it's finished."*

*Joseph smiled contentedly. "Such a good boy. Always such a good boy."*

## About the Author

**Dennis E. Hensley** holds four university degrees in communications, including a PhD in literature and linguistics from Ball State University.

Dr. Hensley is the author of more than fifty books and more than three thousand newspaper and magazine articles, as well as stage plays, film scripts, and songs. He is a professor at Taylor University, where he serves as director of the professional writing major. He and his wife Rose have two grown, married children and four grandchildren.

Dr. Hensley has received numerous honors including the Award for Teaching Excellence by Indiana University, the Elizabeth Sherrill Lifetime Achievement Award by the East Metro Atlanta Christian Writers Association, the Dorothy Hamilton Memorial Writing Award by the Midwest Writers Workshop, and the City of Fort Wayne Bicentennial Gold Medallion. In 2001–02 he was Distinguished Visiting Professor of English and Journalism at the Graduate School of Communication Arts at Regent University. In 2006 he was Distinguished Visiting Lecturer at Oxford University. In 2007 he was Distinguished Visiting Literary Scholar at Moody Bible Institute. He also has received Distinguished Alumnus Awards from T. L. Handy High School, Delta College, and Saginaw Valley

State University. From 1970–71 Dr. Hensley served as a sergeant in the United States Army and was awarded six medals for service in Vietnam.

Research by Dr. Hensley, an academic scholar, has been published in the Pacific Historian, the Ball State University Forum, Echoes, and the Jack London Newsletter. His 600-page opus, The Annotated Edition of Jack London's Martin Eden, was hailed as "a masterpiece of literary analysis" by American Literature Quarterly. He has written six novels, including The Gift (Harvest House); a book on futurism, Millennium Approaches (Avon); several motivation books, such as The Power of Positive Productivity (Possibility Press), and other books on business, finance, communications, public relations, and theology.